THE FROG SURRENDERS

An Amusing & Diverting Account of the Epic Disasters of the French Military

BY
WILLIAM PALAFOX

ILLUSTRATIONS
BY
MARK MARTEL

Copyright © 2013 William Palafox
All rights reserved.
ISBN: 1493602101
ISBN 13: 9781493602100
Library of Congress Control Number: 2013920625
CreateSpace Independent Publishing Platform
North Charleston, South Carolina

Front Cover: *Surrender of Napoleon III on Sepr. 2nd 1870,* George Schlegel, Anne S.K. Brown Military Collection
Back Cover: "A Frenchman weeps as German soldiers march into the French capital, Paris, on June 14, 1940, after the Allied armies had been driven back across France," U.S. National Archives (208-PP-10A-3)

Notice of Political Incorrectness

BEWARE, MORTAL!

What you are about to read runs counter to the tenets of political correctness.

- ❖ Some cultures are presumed to be superior to others.

- ❖ Disparaging remarks are made about a whole host of ethnicities, races, creeds, religions, nationalities, etc.

- ❖ Historical judgments are passed.

- ❖ Feathers are ruffled.

- ❖ Sensitivities are smushed.

For those wishing to file a complaint,
the line to kiss the author's ass forms to the right.

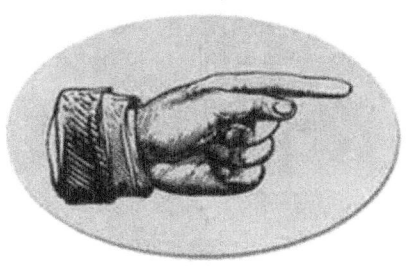

In memory of my father, a great man who had little use for the French

"Tis better using France than trusting France."

—William Shakespeare, *Henry VI*

ACKNOWLEDGMENTS

I would like to thank my lifelong friends, Kirby "Otto" Meade and Herr William Wood, impresario of the Eden War Room, for showing slightly less indifference than all the rest of my acquaintances by pretending to review my work. By valiantly running the spelling and grammar check, they saved me from having to korrect at least a half-duzen minar errers.

Most of all, though, I would like to thank the French people themselves. Without their arrogance and military incompetence, this book would have been impossible and so too would have been my dream of rising from a lowly toll booth attendant to becoming one of the richest men in Possum Creek, Kentucky.

> "France is not inventive, not even in the ranks of error."

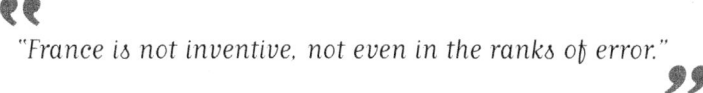

—Vincenzo Gioberti, Italian philosopher, whose heart was in the right place, but did not live long enough to see some pretty inventive French errors

A DEEP, DEEP HISTORICAL MUSING

> "Poor France: it was roughly a hundred years since the country had been torn apart by the Wars of Religion; two centuries back she was being ravaged by the Hundred Years' War. Only one century ahead she would be approaching the chaos of revolution; two centuries on and Paris would be plunged into the bloody insurrection of 1848; three centuries, and the country would barely be recovering from Occupation and Vichy."
>
> — Alistair Horne, *La Belle France* in about as neat a summary as you can get of what a disaster France is

INTRODUCTION

Dear Gentle Reader,

Like so many who were curious enough to pick up a tome subtitled *Epic Disasters of the French Military*, your initial reaction was probably, "Gee, for a book about the French losing wars, it's awfully thin."

The second reaction will reveal a great deal about you, kind bibliophile and patron of the literary arts who undoubtedly purchased this book new instead of resorting to unsavory and unethical practices such as borrowing from a friend or buying used. If you're a real American, you won't need to be sold on the idea that the French are militarily incompetent. You know we bailed their asses out of the last two world wars. Enough said. So, go ahead and buy the book. Atta, boy.

However, if you're one of those squishy products of the weenified American public education system, you're probably asking, "Why pick on the French? They're European and, thus, superior beings." If that's you, allow us to point out that, first, you've got a head full of politically correct, multicultural mush. Second, how's that master's degree in transgendered environmental studies working out for you? Don't worry. Being a barista at Starbucks should get you out from under that $200K mountain of student

debt at about the same time France reconquers Canada. Either way, you desperately need this book.

So, let us answer the question, "Why pick on the French? Why not the Nigerians or the Guatemalans?" The answer is twofold. First, let us freely acknowledge that every nation loses battles and wars. How can we pick on Jacques and *le gang* when the Soviet Union lost in Afghanistan, the United States got run out of Vietnam, and the Germans were trounced in two world wars? The answer is in how you lose.

The Soviets and Americans persisted in unpopular wars for well over a decade. Germany took on all comers and, literally, like a rabid dog, had to be bludgeoned back into its cage. The French, on the other hand, in a span of seventy years—from 1871 to 1940—surrendered their country twice in very brief conflicts and very nearly threw in the towel in a third fight on their home turf.

And so what, you ask? Why not pick on the Poles? They've been run over more times than a speed bump in a parking garage. Simple: the Poles are not and have never been a major power. The French consider themselves one of the world's great cultures and have deluded themselves into believing that they have a military to match. And that is precisely why the French are mocked where the Nigerians and Guatemalans are not. The combined Nigerian/Guatemalan contribution to humanity is zip. No one cares about them (unless, of course, you have been fortunate enough to assist one of the luckless myriad finance officials stranded in Lagos with a paltry $10,000 needing little but your trust and bank account number). The French, on the other hand, have had a major influence on Western civilization—science (Pasteur), mathematics (Pascal), philosophy (Descartes and Rousseau), music (Bizet), and literature (the stuff that you like to read

(Hugo) and the stuff no one reads (Proust)). There is simply no denying the cultural contributions of the French.

France is in the big leagues. They just happen to be the franchise that every AAA club is pretty sure they can beat.

> *"The ignorance of French society gives one a rough sense of the infinite."*
>
> —Ernest Renan, a Frenchman calling it like he saw it

1
THE HIGH WATER MARK — TOURS (732 A.D.)

Caliph Abd-el Melek: "Now tell me about these Franks— what is their nature?"

Musa: "They are a folk right numerous, and full of might: brave and impetuous in the attack, but cowardly and craven in the event of defeat."

Pity the poor Caliph of Baghdad. For a hundred years on, the Arab Empire had taken the world by storm, spreading their annoying religion of Islam like equally annoying Starbucks franchises. Turban futures stood at an all-time high, the fall line of burkas showed a scandalous amount of forehead, but now disturbing news reached him that, near a small village in the distant land of the cowardly and craven Franks, his army had been thoroughly routed and its commander, Abd al-Rahman, killed. He could not know it at the moment, but his realm had reached its high water mark.

Very little is known of the Battle of Tours. Some historians snottily refer to it as the Battle of Poitiers, but, since no one is even sure where the battlefield is, who are they to monkey with such a time-honored tradition? What we do know is that an Arab army, numbering between sixty thousand to four hundred thousand men (see how little we know?), advanced into France out of Spain in search of the cheap wine and skanky women for which France is still known to this very day. Many scholars will drone on pointlessly about spreading Islam, conquering territory, plundering, blah, blah, blah. However, as we will see in future chapters, everyone comes to France for the wine and the women. Otherwise, the place is useless to us.

Not content with Muslim thugs running loose in his land, an attitude sorely lacking in later generations of Frenchmen, Charles Martel, leader of the Austrasian Franks, and his army met the Arab horde near Tours or Poitiers or wherever. Since we're short on details, the only thing we do know is that Martel and company won big, earning him the very cool nickname of Charles the Hammer. Later estimates would put the number of Arab dead at 375,000, which would seem impossible if only sixty thousand of them were involved. This sort of exaggeration should come as no surprise from a people who claimed to have helped win World War II.

A plausible explanation for the lack of information on this important battle, which Edward Creasy includes in his famous *Fifteen Decisive Battles of the World,* is that the incredible shock of seeing a French army victorious killed every literate human capable of recording the events of the day.

Clearly, if Charles Martel had known what the future held for his martial descendants, he would have erected a very large, very obvious monument on the spot of his greatest triumph. Never since that long-ago October day have the French won a significant outright and enduring military victory

on their own. Of course, the little tidbit that Charles's son was named Pippin the Short should have been a fair hint of what was to come.

So, let us all start out by freely acknowledging that we owe the French a big one on this. Without them, perhaps, all our women would be in burkas and all our men in turbans. And this'll, hopefully, be the last positive thing said about the French in this book.

"The decline of the French monarchy invited the attack of these insatiate fanatics. The descendants of Clovis had lost the inheritance of his martial and ferocious spirit; and their misfortune or demerit has affixed the epithet of lazy to the last kings of the Merovingian race. They ascended the throne without power, and sunk into the grave without a name. . . . The vineyards of Gascony and the city of Bordeaux were possessed by the sovereign of Damascus and Samarkand; and the south of France, from the mouth of the Garonne to that of the Rhone, assumed the manners and religion of Arabia."

—Edward Gibbon, *The History of the Decline and Fall of the Roman Empire*, though it's uncertain as to whether he was recounting the history of the 8th century or predicting the future of the 21st

They could save a lot of money if they stopped paying people to surrender.
—Oscar Wilde

2
WHAT'S IN A NAME?

France wasn't always France, and the French weren't always French. However, we think we have a pretty good angle on when all the fun started. Try to keep up.

Sometime late in the waning days of the Roman Empire, around 355 A.D., a Germanic tribe called the Franks (you see where this is going, right?) crossed into Roman territory from Frisia (where the Netherlands is today) to serve as *foederati*, an allied tribe. Basically, they were barbarians who had been crashing the Latin party for over a century with border incursions. Tired of the unseemly mayhem, the Romans offered these unwelcome houseguests a deal: serve as soldiers, don't monkey with our trade to Britain, and we'll all pretend this was on the up and up. The Franks agreed, called their new digs Francia, and everyone was happy. As you will recall, our good friend Charles Martel, who we met in the last chapter bashing Muslim skulls, was an Austrasian Frank. Austrasia (not Australia) is now the eastern part of France.

So, it's pretty simple: German-speaking Germans who fought like Germans moved into what became German territory. And ever since, the Germans have wanted it back. The French, undoubtedly as confused by this ancestral conundrum as a collegiate football player in a physics class, have played the wine-swilling battered wife to Germany's beer-besotted angry husband ever since.

Of course, the question still remains: How did these fierce, horned-helmet wearing, warring tribal Germans become soft beret-wearing, capitulating, café-dwelling Frenchmen?

Unfortunately, there is no scientific explanation that can be offered, but the following is probably as close to the truth as we will ever know:

> *"The Franks had all been Germans at first, but some of them had taken to eating frogs and snails and were gradually turned into Frenchmen, a fact not generally known at the time because there were no French as yet."*
>
> — Will Cuppy, *The Decline and Fall of Practically Everybody*

3
HOW TO BE A GREAT FRENCH MILITARY COMMANDER

1. Don't be French—the Napoléon Rule

2. Don't be a man (in the literal biological sense, not the figurative "Don't be a sissy" sense)—the Joan of Arc Rule

3. Don't fight the Germans—the Otto von Bismarck Rule

4. Have Americans on your side—the George S. Patton Rule

5. Fight other Frenchmen—the Robespierre Rule

6. Never ever fight the Germans—the Adolph Hitler Rule

7. Avoid Moscow—the other Napoléon Rule

8. Build massive fortifications along the German border. The Germans would never violate the neutrality of Belgium and… oops, never mind—The Maginot Rule (cancelled May 1940)

9. Whatever you do, don't fight the Germans—the von Moltke Rule

10. Invade hellish sub-Saharan African countries. Bribe locals. Force natives to speak French. Point to the 3.7 percent literacy rate as proof of the glory of France—The Lyautey Rule

<u>Bonus Post-Modern Rule</u>
11. Remind oneself that concepts such as "victory" and "defeat" are merely social constructs, according to Foucault. If one feels that one is winning, then, *eh bien,* one is winning, *non?*—the Derrida Rule

❝ "France always has plenty of men of talent, but it is always deficient in men of action and high character." ❞

—Napoléon Bonaparte

4
THE SIGNS WERE THERE EARLY ON

Like much of Europe in the eighth through eleventh centuries, the Franks had to deal with those fun-loving marauders, the Vikings (before they moved to Minnesota to play a brand of listless football more suggestive of France than Norseland). One of the most famous of these Norsemen was Hrolf Ganger, better known to history as Rollo (yup, that Hrolf Ganger). Rollo/Hrolf was part of a Viking fleet that sailed up the Seine and laid siege to Paris in November 885. Rollo liked France so much that he returned the next year and invaded Normandy. Now, normally, the Vikings were in it for the loot, and, once they grabbed everything worth hauling off, they skedaddled. But not this time. No, our buddy Rollo was here for keeps (see: women and wine), and the Franks, beginning to show the worrisome signs of becoming French, did nothing about it.

Trying to make the best of an awful situation, King Charles the Simple (now there's a man to rally 'round) gave Rollo the land around Rouen on condition that the Vikings convert to Christianity and defend the realm

against other Vikings who were late to the party. Rollo agreed to the generous terms.

In 911, the two parties agreed to the Treaty of Saint-Clair-sur-Epte. Rollo got the hand of Gisele (and presumably the rest of her as well, though one shouldn't assume anything; those were brutal times back then), Charles's illegitimate daughter, for good measure. However, there was one last complication. Technically, Rollo was now the vassal of his new (simple) king, which meant he would have to kneel and kiss Charles's foot. Rollo would have none of that kneeling nonsense; after all, he was the winner here. So, in the spirit of compromise—which was, after all, the hallmark of the great Viking warriors, amicable chaps that they were—Rollo agreed to kiss Charles's foot from a standing position. Chuck had to lift his foot so high that he lost his balance and fell over.

Another great moment in French history.

"France has neither winter nor summer nor morals. Apart from these drawbacks it is a fine country."

—Mark Twain

The Viking Rollo agrees to become a vassal of King Charles the Simple and kiss his foot.

5

LES EXPOS

They were arguably the worst franchise to ever play major league baseball. [The Washington Senators (first in war, first in peace, last in the American League) did at least manage three World Series appearances and won the whole shebang in 1924.]

In thirty-six seasons, this cursed franchise managed just one playoff appearance. Their greatest season ever was preempted by a labor strike in 1994. They almost always had the lowest attendance in the league. Their mascot, Youppi, was the ugliest creature to ever infest a ball park. Players insisted on no-trade clauses that prevented them from being relegated to this baseball backwater and never met any resistance on the point. Worst of all, the franchise produced some high-quality talent that was always looking to flee for its professional life. They always looked better on paper than they played on the field. Something that dysfunctional just had French written all over it, and, with that hint, you probably guessed we were talking about the Montreal Expos. (Of course, the chapter title probably gave it away.)

Just as the French Army is out of its depth in the German game of war, so were the Montreal Expos just as out of place in the American game of baseball. Go Nationals!

For those of you who enjoy watching train wrecks, here's the tale of the tape on the woeful history of Les Expos:

SEASON	W	L	PCT
1969	52	110	0.321
1970	73	89	0.451
1971	71	90	0.441
1972	70	86	0.449
1973	79	83	0.488
1974	79	82	0.491
1975	75	87	0.463
1976	55	107	0.34
1977	75	87	0.463
1978	76	86	0.469
1979	95	65	0.594
1980	90	72	0.556
1981	60	48	0.556
1982	86	76	0.531
1983	82	80	0.506
1984	78	83	0.484
1985	84	77	0.522
1986	78	83	0.484
1987	91	71	0.562
1988	81	81	0.5
1989	81	81	0.5
1990	85	77	0.525
1991	71	90	0.441
1992	87	75	0.537
1993	94	68	0.58

SEASONS	WINS	LOSSES	PCT.
1994	74	40	0.649
1995	66	78	0.458
1996	88	74	0.543
1997	78	84	0.481
1998	65	97	0.401
1999	68	94	0.42
2000	67	95	0.414
2001	68	94	0.42
2002	83	79	0.512
2003	83	79	0.512
2004	67	95	0.414
SEASONS	WINS	LOSSES	PCT.
36	2755	2943	0.484

Now, let's have a look at the uncannily similar record of the Montreal Expos' AAA farm team back in the home country:

CONFLICT	YEAR	OUTCOME	COMMENTARY
Arab Invasion	732	W	Charles Martel declares: "I, for one, will not wear a turban!"
Viking Invasion	845 – 911	L	Vikings come a-calling and decide to stay in Normandy.
First Crusade	1096-1099	W	Pope Urban II has brilliant idea: kill Muslims and get rid of surplus French knights all at one great, low price. All are greatly surprised when the hare-brained scheme actually captures Jerusalem.
Second Crusade	1147-1149	L	French travel to Damascus, quarrel, fail to capture Damascus, give up, go home.

Third Crusade	1189-1192	L	Richard the Lion-Hearted learns the First Rule of Being a Great English Commander: Never Ally with the French. That's pretty much the First Rule for Being a Great Commander in any country (including France).
Fourth Crusade	1202-1204	L	Perhaps a bit uncertain as to the goal of the Crusades or perhaps looking ahead to its eventual Turkish occupation, French attack and capture the non-Muslim city of Constantinople.
Angevin-Flanders War	1202-1214	W	England's King John loses so much respect after being defeated by the French that his nobles force him to sign the Magna Carta.
Albegensian Crusade	1209-1229	W	Not having much luck with infidels in the eastern Mediterranean, the French decide to stay home and butcher their own homegrown heretics, the Cathars.
Seventh Crusade	1248-1254	L	Louis IX gets that crusading feeling, but the Muslims are ready for him, as the annual arrival of crusaders was somewhat akin to the swallows returning to San Juan Capistrano.
Eighth Crusade	1267-1270	L	Eighth Crusade, same as the Seventh. A little bit louder, a lotta bit worse, especially for Louis IX, who dies from disease.
Flanders Invasion	1302	L	Those Flemish peasants are tougher than they look. So many French knights are killed at the Battle of Courtrai that it's often called the Battle of the Golden Spurs from the large number of spurs collected from the dead bodies.

War	Dates	Result	Description
Hundred Years' War	1337-1453	W	English battle Scots, Welsh, Irish, themselves, French, crappy food, bad weather. Make decisive mistake of allying with some French against other French.
Italian Wars	1495-1515	L	Italy part of France? Perish the thought.
Habsburg-Valois Wars	1522-1559	Draw	Francis I takes on the Holy Roman Emperor Charles V. Of course, the fact that Charles is also duking it out with the Turks, Germans, the Protestant Reformation, the Pope, the Italians, and the Comanches (okay, maybe not them) has nothing to do with the French decision to make a (mainly unsuccessful) land grab.
Religious Wars	1559-1598	Draw	French Catholics versus French Protestants. What tolerance! What diversity! What bloodshed!
Thirty Years' War	1618-1648	W	Cardinal Richelieu sides with the Protestants of Sweden and the Netherlands against his co-religionists in Spain and Germany. Somehow Sweden with a fifth of the population conquers more turf than the Frogs.
War of Devolution	1667-1668	Draw	Louis XIV likes the look of the Spanish Netherlands. The Spanish, Dutch and English don't like the sound of the "French" Netherlands.
Franco-Dutch War	1672-1678	Draw	Louis XIV gains Franche Comte, but what he really, really wanted was to conquer the cursed Dutch.
War of the Reunions	1683-1684	W	All of this? Over Luxembourg? Oh, the humanity.

Nine Years' War	1688-1697	L	Call it the War of the League of Augsburg. Or the War of the Grand Alliance. Or perhaps the Orleans War. Or maybe the War of the Palatinian Succession. How about the War of the English Succession? Just don't call it a French victory.
War of the Spanish Succession	1701-1714	L	A dead Spanish king provokes a feeding frenzy amongst European royalty. France gets the scraps.
War of the Quadruple Alliance	1718-1720	W	Spain versus Britain, Austria, the Netherlands, and, ah yes, France. Royal Navy does all the heavy lifting. French sneer that they would have done better, if they had a navy.
War of the Polish Succession	1733-1738	W	The French finally win one of these Succession Wars and end up with Lorraine.
War of the Austrian Succession	1740-1748	Draw	A most unnatural war where France and Prussia are allied.
French-Indian War	1754-1763	L	A military match made in hell. Indians can't hold their liquor. French can't hold their positions. Britain relieves France of the burden of dealing with Canada. French lose interest in hockey.
Seven Years' War	1756-1763	L	Prussians decide to fight everyone on the continent simultaneously. The British opt to do the same at sea. France gets pasted everywhere by everyone.
American Revolution	1778-1783	W	Lafayette learns Rule #4 of Being a Great French Commander.
French Revolution	1789-1799	Draw	Angry, smelly French defeat corrupt, smelly French. Louis XVI misplaces his head. For some reason, the world isn't amused.

Haitian Revolution	1791-1804	L	Yellow Fever and Toussaint L'Ouverture are too much for the Frogs.
Quasi War	1798-1800	L	French privateers raid American commerce. Americans wake up, finally understanding that Frogs can't be trusted as far as you can throw them, build a navy, defeat French.
Napoleonic Wars	1799-1815	L	Corsican-born Italian dictator accomplishes amazing task of making just about everyone forget that they were fighting against the French. The British aren't fooled. Lot of style points, but a loss is still a loss.
Algeria	1830-1847	W	France brings civilization to Algeria, which included copious amounts of raping and looting. That'll learn those ignorant savages.
Pastry War	1838	W	A French pastry chef in Mexico?
First Franco-Moroccan War	1844	W	Algerian rebels find sanctuary in Morocco; French forces follow in pursuit
Crimean War	1854-1856	W	French team up with British to save the Turkish from the Russians. French incompetence rubs off on all parties.
Second Opium War	1856-1860	W	French sign up with British to force Chinese to buy opium. Nice going.
Austro-Sardinian War	1859	Draw	French armies beat the hell out of the Austrians, but Italians scoop up all the territory.
Mexican Intervention	1862-1867	L	Deadbeat Mexicans forego paying their loans and end up with French occupiers and an Austrian puppet emperor. What could possibly go wrong?

Franco-Prussian War	1870-1871	L	Napoléon III forgets Rule #1 about being a Great French Commander. Hell, he violated just about all the rules.
Sino-French War	1884-1885	Draw	France spars with China, but loses its shirt
First Mandingo War	1883-1886	Draw	The Scramble for Africa is on and France has its eye on West Africa. Most history books say the French won this, but why did they have to come back less than a decade later?
First Franco-Dahomean War	1890	Draw	The Frogs get a favorable treaty, but both sides gear up for Round Two.
Second Franco-Dahomean War	1892-1894	W	On the other hand, the Dahomeans are considered to be the French of West Africa.
Second Mandingo War	1894-1895	L	Samori Ture sends the French packing…for a few years.
Madagascar	1895-1896	W	French save the world from the threat of Malagasy hegemony.
Third Mandingo War	1898	W	A game fight, but cannons finally trump spears.
Second Franco-Moroccan War	1911-1912	W	France finally subdues the last independent land in North Africa, sorta, kinda.
World War I	1914-1918	W	Being on the winning side helps, but it's hard to overlook the Great Mutiny of 1917.
Zaian War	1914-1921	L	Frogs never do manage to suppress this rebellion by the Berbers in the mountains of Morocco.

World War II	1939-1940	L	Phony War turns real in a big hurry. Hitler declares: I love Paree!
Vietnam War	1946-1954	L	Ho Chi Minh says, "Better Red than French." The United States should have paid a lot more attention.
Algerian War	1954-1962	L	Algeria will always be a part of France. Or maybe not.
Suez Crisis	1956-1957	L	Egypt grabs Suez Canal. France, Great Britain and Israel grab Egypt. US and USSR make 'em spit it back out.
<u>WINS</u>	<u>LOSSES</u>	<u>DRAWS</u>	<u>PCT.</u>
<u>20</u>	<u>23</u>	<u>10</u>	<u>0.472</u>

❝
"They're only interested in three things: the best place to eat, having sex, and how quickly they can run away. Much like the French."
❞

—Ted Nugent, rock star, philosopher and keen observer of the habits of deer, elk, and other tasty woodland creatures

6

HISTORY'S FIRST CATASTROPHIC FRENCH DEFEAT

Fight:	Battle of Hattin
Date:	July 4, 1187
Opponents:	French Crusaders versus Ayyubid Arabs
Incompetent French Leader:	Guy of Lusignan, King of Jerusalem
Outcome:	Horrendous French Defeat

THE PATHETIC DETAILS:

As previously discussed, at some point in time, the Franks who came west of the Rhine stopped being German and became French. It's a hard thing to put your finger on, and there's no point in droning on about Merovingians and Carolingians and Capetians. No, at some point, the French became the French, and probably the best way to figure out when that was is to find a battle where they did something really stupid, lost big and couldn't recover. Sounds like a textbook definition of being French to us.

In this day and age, most folks don't realize that the Crusades were mainly a French-dominated affair. The pope who thought up the entire idea: Urban II, Frenchman. Most of the knights: French. The backbiting that took place: pure *française*. The long string of demoralizing losses: *Vive la France!* However, after numerous misfires and much to everyone's surprise, the First Crusade culminated with the capture of Jerusalem in July 1099.

The crusaders broke up the Holy Land into several "Crusader states," such as Antioch, Edessa, Jerusalem, and Tripoli. Jerusalem, given its spiritual role, was the centerpiece, and Godfrey of Bouillon became its first ruler, though he modestly insisted on being known as the Defender of the Holy Sepulcher. This modesty did not pass on to his successors, who preferred the punchier title of "King of Jerusalem."

Eventually, the title ended up in the hands of one Guy of Lusignan, born in 1150 in Poitou, thanks to his marriage to Sibylla, daughter of King Amalric I, and the untimely death of her nine-year-old son, Baldwin V, in 1186.

Now, Guy was a newcomer to his kingdom and immediately rubbed the "native" crusaders the wrong way. The natives wanted peace with the surrounding Muslims, who were led by the highly capable Salah ad-Din Yusuf Ibn Ayyub, or, as he is better known to history, Saladin the Kurdish-born Sultan of Egypt. This native faction was typified by Raymond III, Count of Tripoli. However, Guy and his crowd were there to hack and slash and win war spoils.

A year into Guy's reign, he had an all-out fight on his hands with Saladin. Raymond, who had already made a separate peace with Saladin, decided his best chances in the conflict stood with Guy. Raymond's decision prompted Saladin to besiege the Count's fortress at Tiberias where

Raymond's wife was trapped inside. The crusaders raised an army of over one thousand knights and twenty thousand infantry to relieve the siege. Raymond advised against a march on Tiberias, arguing that this reaction was precisely what Saladin wanted since the army would be forced to march in the summer heat with no access to water. Guy's cronies accused the prudent count of cowardice. So strong is the Frenchman's aversion to water that he, occasionally, deludes himself into thinking that the liquid substance has no use whatsoever.

What ensued was a disaster of epic proportions. The route of march from Acre to Tiberias was devoid of watering holes, and the Crusaders were harassed mercilessly by the Arab cavalry. By the end of the day on July 3, the Crusaders were trapped on an open plain, completely surrounded. Ominously, the men and horses had not taken water in a full day.

On the morning of July 4, desperate with thirst, the army tried to break through Saladin's lines toward the springs at Hattin. Eventually, almost the entire Crusader army was forced onto two knobby hills known as the Horns of Hattin. After several futile attempts at a breakout, the Crusaders surrendered. Guy was captured and treated respectfully by Saladin.

The aftermath of the battle was even worse for the Crusader cause. Guy and Raymond had stripped virtually every castle in the region to fully man the army that was destroyed at Hattin. Saladin rolled up the Crusader states and recaptured Jerusalem on October 2. All of the hard work done by the First Crusade had been undone in a single afternoon. How very French.

> "We can stand here like the French, or we can do something about it."
>
> — Marge Simpson, *The Simpsons*

Battle of Hattin as depicted in "Passages faiz oultre mer par les François contre les Turcqs et autres Sarrazins et Mores oultre marins"

7
LE VOCABULAIRE

Essential Military Term	**En Français**
Defeat	Défaite
Victory	Pas de défaite
Army	Foule paniquard (literally, panic-stricken mob)
Soldier	Captif de guerre
Rifle	Une chose pesant que retarder la retraite (lit., heavy thing that impedes retreat)
Retreat	Retraite
Disaster	Désastre
Catastrophe	Catastrophe
Surrender	Capitulation
Debacle	Débâcle (and you thought you didn't know any French)
Scapegoat	Juif
Alliance	Relations nécessaire pour sauver Paris

False sense of confidence	Maginot
Looter	Pillard
Straggler	Traînard
Battalion	Groupe des pillardes et traînardes
Logistics	Vin et fromage (wine and cheese)
Collapse	Effondrement (leave it to the French to make something awful sound so sexy)
POW camp	Chez Français
American	Idiot
English	Idiot
Belgian	Idiot
Russian	Idiot
African	Idiot
Asian	Idiot
German	Idiot dangereux
Cower	Trembler comme un Français
Ship	Piège fatal flottant (lit., floating death trap)
Tank	Piège fatal blinde (lit., armored death trap)
Airplane	Piège fatal volant (you get the picture)
Outflanked	Pas encore (lit., not again)
Surrounded	Pas encore

> "The French constitute the most brilliant and the most dangerous nation in Europe and the best qualified in turn to become an object of admiration, hatred, pity or terror but never indifference."
>
> —Alexis de Tocqueville

8
HISTORY'S FIRST ANNOYING FRENCHMAN

Name: **Raynald of Chatillon**
Conflict: **Crusades**
Opponent: **Saladin**
Notable Catastrophe: **Battle of Hattin**

THE DREARY DETAILS:

Let us start this section on a French crusader by noting that everyone loves the Chicago Cubs (unless you're a Chicago White Sox fan), and everybody hates the French (unless you're French). Both are historical losers, but the former bring a warm smile to the baseball fan's face. The latter are despised by enemy and ally alike.

Why the difference?

One may suspect that it has to do with humility. The Cubs have been, are, and will continue to be awful. They freely acknowledge it. Their fans readily admit it. They lose when they have talent. They lose when they have no talent. Sometimes, there is a faint need to pin blame on a goat that was denied entry to a game long ago, but, for the most part, the Cubs are like your dopey uncle who drives delivery for the local pizza joint: modest, loveable, doesn't offer his two cents on things he doesn't understand, usually drunk, often forgets to wear trousers in public.

Of course, the French are the exact opposite (except for the drunk part). They are like you next-door neighbor's kid who just failed out of community college from too much angst and amphetamines and is now living in the basement. He's scrawny, opinionated, degenerate, intelligent, talented, amoral, and untrustworthy. He has a high opinion of himself and sneers at you as you drive off to your silly, little job to feed your petty, bourgeois existence.

And just like France, you'd love to kick his ass, but there's no need because the local high school kids do the job for you on a fairly regular basis.

Where the heck were we?

Ah, yes. Raynald of Chatillon is possibly the first historical character that we can point our finger at and say, "Now, that is a Frenchman!"

Raynald was born in 1125 in the Champagne region of the same noble family that produced Pope Urban II, who gave us the Crusades. Raynald was an ambitious young fellow who joined the Second Crusade, where he found his way to Antioch and married far above his station in 1153 to become the Prince of Antioch.

Wasting little time, he tried to extort money from the Byzantine Emperor Manuel I Comnenus and attacked the island of Cyprus when payment was not forthcoming. Raynald's little expedition of rape and pillage did not amuse the Emperor, who marched into Syria at the head of an army. Raynald was forced to beg for his very life, barefoot and in sackcloth, before Manuel's throne. As a nice little touch, the Emperor had Raynald lead his horse into Antioch when he came to visit Baldwin III in 1159.

That twisted combination of viciousness and groveling can usually only be found in the French.

The next year, much to everyone's profound relief, Raynald was captured by the Arabs during a raid and spent the next seventeen years as a prisoner until someone got around to paying his ransom, reputed to be 120,000 gold dinars, which sounds like a lot of money for a useless Frenchman.

Raynald returned to the free world in a foul mood, no doubt. However, in 1177, he still had sufficient charm to marry yet another wealthy widow—this time, the alluring Stephanie, who had survived both Humphrey III of Toron and Miles of Plancy. Raynald probably didn't understand that two data points make a trend, but, understandably, he was distracted by the fact that, along with Stephanie's hand, he was also receiving the realm of Oultrejordain.

This now put Raynald across the trade routes that ran between Egypt and Syria, which was obviously not a good thing for a man like him. Despite a truce between Salah ad-Din Yusuf Ibn Ayyub (Saladin) and Baldwin IV, Raynald ran amok, plundering caravans, threatening Mecca, engaging in piracy on the Red Sea, and generally just making a nuisance out of himself (in short, being French). Saladin took all of this with his usual aplomb and besieged Raynald in his castle at Kerak during his son's wedding. Taking the hint, Raynald quieted down and remained so until 1186.

Unfortunately, at that time, turmoil over the succession for the kingship in Jerusalem let the Raynald out of the bottle. When Raynald's forces attacked a caravan that Saladin's sister was riding in, the gloves finally came off. Saladin swore he would have Raynald's head, and, after the disastrous Battle of Hattin (Chapter 7), he got his chance. Let us enjoy Raynald's final moments as related by the Arab chronicler Imad al-Din:

Saladin invited the king [Guy] to sit beside him, and when Arnat [Raynald] entered in his turn, he seated him next to his king and reminded him of his misdeeds.

"How many times have you sworn an oath and violated it? How many times have you signed agreements you have never respected?"

Raynald answered through a translator: "Kings have always acted thus. I did nothing more."

During this time King Guy was gasping with thirst, his head dangling as though drunk, his face betraying great fright. Saladin spoke reassuring words to him, had cold water brought, and offered it to him. The king drank, then handed what remained to Raynald, who slaked his thirst in turn. The sultan then said to Guy: "You did not ask permission before giving him water. I am therefore not obliged to grant him mercy."

After pronouncing these words, the sultan smiled, mounted his horse, and rode off, leaving the captives in terror. He supervised the return of the troops, and then came back to his tent. He ordered Raynald brought there, then advanced before him, sword in hand, and struck him between the neck and the shoulder blade. When Raynald fell, he cut off his head and dragged the body by its feet to the king, who began to tremble. Seeing him thus upset, Saladin said to him in a reassuring tone: "This man was killed only because of his malfeasance and perfidy."

That Saladin. What a guy. Adieu, Raynald.

❝
"The French are a smallish, monkey-looking bunch and not dressed any better, on average, than the citizens of Baltimore. True, you can sit outside in Paris and drink little cups of coffee, but why this is more stylish than sitting inside and drinking large glasses of whiskey, I don't know."
❞

—P. J. O'Rourke, *Holidays in Hell*

9
FACT OR FICTION?

1. French tanks only have one gear—reverse.

   FALSE. French tanks also have a forward gear because being attacked from behind is quite common.

2. French officers used to wear red uniforms to conceal the blood from their wounds from their men.

   FALSE. They wore brown trousers.

3. French sailors have to be taller than six feet.

   FALSE. This myth evolved from the untruth that the sailors had to be of a particular height, so they could walk ashore when their ships sank in the harbor. However, the truth is that they can usually step out onto the pier as their vessels take the final plunge (see Chapter 41, The Curious Case of the French Battleships).

4. The French heroically conquered a major city during the Fourth Crusade.

   FACT. Unfortunately, Constantinople belonged to their supposed allies, the Byzantine Greeks.

5. The Arc de Triomphe in Paris has never been used for a military victory parade.

   FALSE. The German Army has used it several times.

6. Forty million Frenchmen can't be wrong.

   FACT. They can be defeated, humiliated, abused, taught to sing the "Horst Wessel" song, coerced into bathing at least once a month, but they can't be wrong. No siree, Bob.

7. Without the French, there would be no cure for rabies.

   FACT. But we were willing to live with that tradeoff.

8. The French Navy is greatly feared.

   FACT. Particularly by its own sailors.

9. French fighter planes are codenamed "Mirage."

   FACT. If you're in a dogfight and think you saw a French airplane in it, it had to have been a mirage.

10. French women are notorious for dispensing sexual favors to foreign soldiers.

    FACT. Everyone prefers to sleep with a winner, even if he calls her *fraulein*.

11. The French decry American influences like McDonald's and EuroDisney.

    FACT. They've put up a stronger fight against hamburgers than they did against the Nazis, but, after all these years, they have yet to subdue an unarmed mouse.

12. The French Foreign Legion will enlist murderers, thieves, rapists, con artists, and every other sort of vile criminal into its ranks.

    FACT. But if you're a French citizen and wish to join, you must use a false name, which ought to tell you something.

13. Fireworks are forbidden at EuroDisney.

    FACT. The Disney Company got tired of processing all the French tourists who kept surrendering.

14. The French military has the most extensive language training in the world.

    FACT. They must be prepared to surrender fluently anywhere in the world.

15. Secret French Army plans have over one hundred thousand men defending Paris in case of invasion.

    FALSE. The French Army has never tried to defend Paris.

> "Oh, French people, how frivolous you are! You show us the leash and you prove that you need to be led…"
>
> —Madame de Sade

10

HOW TO BE A GREAT FRENCH SOLDIER

1. You run faster *without* the rifle.

2. White wine goes best with surrender.

3. If you are feeling homesick, just remember that your family back *chez vous* is doing their best to collaborate with the enemy as well.

4. Take the initiative! If your unit commander hasn't already surrendered, do so yourself.

5. If taunted by Americans after being rescued from a POW camp, remind yourself that, unlike the idiot Yanks, you have never and will never eat processed cheese.

6. If the army wanted you to have a mistress, you would have been issued one, which is why you have been issued one.

7. Your ability to eat snails and frogs makes you a natural for fleeing through the backwoods.

> "A Frenchman loves his king as he loves his Mistress to madness, because he thinks it is great and noble to be mad."

—Gouverneur Morris

11
MILITARY MOTTOES FROM AROUND THE GLOBE

Semper Fidelis (Always Faithful)—U. S. Marine Corps
Semper Paratus (Always Ready)—U. S. Coast Guard
Who Dares, Wins—British Special Air Service
Not By Strength, But By Guile—British Special Boat Service
To The First Breakwater…and No Further—French Navy
Qua Patet Orbis (As Far As The World Extends)—Royal Dutch Marines (fairly aggressive statement for a country the size of Rhode Island, but, then again, *Qua Patet Luxembourg* doesn't quite ring)
"We Won't Fight. You Can't Make Us."—French Army
"We Won't Lead. You Can't Make Us."—French Staff College

> "Like a Frenchman quaking in a thunderstorm."
>
> — Al Bundy, *Married with Children*

The French Coat of Arms

12

THE HUNDRED AND SIXTEEN YEARS' WAR

Conflict: Hundred Years' War
Date: 1337 - 1453
Opponents: French versus English
Incompetent French Leader: So many, it wouldn't be fair to single out just one
Outcome: French lose almost all the battles, win the war (Oh, that was painful to write.)

THE PATHETIC DETAILS:

It all started when William got bored back in 1066 and conquered England (see Chapter 13). He wasn't French, but nobility on both sides of the English Channel ended up related to each other. And, then, one day in 1328, lo and behold, Charles IV, last of the Capetians (not Mohicans), died without so much as leaving a single male heir behind. Of course, you probably already figured out that the closest male relative lived across the way in fair England. That would have been Edward III, King of England.

Now, as much as all decent, hard-working, sober people detest the French, it's hard to blame them for not wanting to hand over the keys of the realm to an Englishman. They hunted around and found just the right man—one still upright with a pulse and most of his teeth. That was none other than Philip of Valois (P to the V, to his buds), whose claim to the throne passed through his father Charles, who was the son of Philip III, who had been the king from 1270-1285. Edward III dismissed that claim as being as outlandish as a soap opera plot. The fight was on.

Obviously, a conflict named the Hundred Years' War, which was actually 116 years long, had its ups and downs. The English invariably fought outnumbered and also had to contend with simultaneous scrums in Scotland and Spain (ah, sweet alliteration, a sign of literature of the highest order, which this tome is). Even worse, they made the unpardonable sin of allying with the Burgundian French against the Armagnac French. If you learn nothing else from this book, walk away with this: NEVER SIDE WITH THE FRENCH! Even if you're French. Even if you're fighting other French.

So, despite crushing, demoralizing, jaw-dropping defeats at Sluys (1340) (giving the Frog Navy a taste of what the future held for them), Crecy (1346), Poitiers (1356), and Agincourt (1415) (see below), the French finally turned the home field to their advantage and drove the English out in 1453 after the Battle of Castillon.

NOTABLE CATASTROPHE:

When someone writes a play about a battle, you know it didn't turn out well for someone. Not surprisingly, the someones in this case were the French.

It was late 1415, and Henry V of England (Hank Sank to those with a clever sense of word play) was in deep trouble. His army had been whittled down by hunger and disease, and the campaign itself had not netted much. As he retreated toward his only safe haven in France, Calais on the Channel, a French army led by Charles d'Albret, Constable of France, skillfully blocked his path. Henry did not wish to battle with his weakened force, but, if he did not reach Calais, the elements and sickness would destroy his army.

Now to hear Shakespeare tell it, Henry and his band of brothers were outnumbered about one hundred to one, but modern research suggests it was about three to two odds, still a daunting task for a diminished army far from base as the opponents squared off on St. Crispin's Day, October 25, 1415.

To say the fight did not go well for the French (and they rarely do) would be a monumental understatement. The battlefield itself was narrow, which prevented the French from using their numerical superiority. A heavy rain the night before had turned the ground into a muddy mess that slowed the progress of the armored knights. As they tried to close the English position, they were pelted by arrows from the longbowmen stationed in advance of the main line. By the time they made it into slugging range, the French formation had degenerated into a chaotic mob, unable to maneuver (see John Keegan's *Face of Battle* for a description of this mosh pit of death), easy pickings for the unarmored English infantry, who swooped in through the gaps in the lines and stabbed and hacked where the knights' armor was weakest.

When the fight was done, five thousand noblemen lay dead, including Constable D'Albret, and nearly a hundred dukes, counts, and barons. Normally, the English would have just captured the nobility and ransomed them off, but, still outnumbered despite the victory, Henry V ordered the prisoners executed after his baggage train was attacked.

With the win at Agincourt, Henry went from rags to riches (and literary immortality, courtesy of the Bard). By the Treaty of Troyes signed in 1420, he was made regent and heir to the French throne. He also married Catherine of Valois, daughter of Charles VI (current French king at the time, if you're keeping score at home). However, Henry would be dead in two years, never to combine the kingdoms of England and France, saving the English from generations of wimpy behavior.

> "He [Henry II of England] has everything in abundance—men, horses, gold, silk, diamonds, game and fruit. We in France, we have only bread, wine—and gaiety."
>
> — Louis VII (or VIII or IX or CLXVI, hard to keep up with all those darn Louises)

13

MYTH BUSTER #1

Myth: There are a lot of French words in the English language because the French conquered the English way back when.

Truth: Wrong! If you're walking around with that notion in your skull, you obviously went to a public school in the United States or are a degenerate Frenchman. Far better to be completely ignorant of history than to remember one iota of the PC multi-culti rubbish that is vomited up in American classrooms.

As we were saying, all this confusion about French and English comes from the Norman Conquest of 1066 when William the Conqueror (obviously, he won with that sobriquet) defeated Harold Godwinson at Hastings. Notice we said *Norman* Conquest. Not French Conquest or Pastry Chef Conquest or Annoying Mime Conquest. Normans. From Normandy. Which is in France. But the Normans were Vikings (Normans = Norseman, got it?) who decided they liked easy access to French wine and English food. The very same Vikings who arrived in 911 under Rollo the Viking and incorporated aspects of the French language into their own. But they weren't Frogs. So there.

> "A barbarous country where the houses were gloomy, the churches ugly and the customs revolting."
>
> — Anne of Kiev, in a letter to her father, Yaroslav the Great in 1051, extolling the virtues of La Belle France

14

NEVER TRUST THE FRENCH...
ESPECIALLY IF YOU'RE FRENCH

Name:	Jeanne d'Arc (Joan of Arc) (1412-1431)
Conflict:	Hundred Years' War
Opponent:	English and Burgundian French
Notable Catastrophe:	Getting Burned at the Stake

THE DREARY DETAILS:

Joan is one of the great figures in French history, which is understandable, given that she fulfilled Rules #2, 3, 5, 6, 7 and 9 back in Chapter 3. It's also pretty telling about a nation's military when a teenage girl prone to hallucinations has to pull its collective fat out of the fire. That would be like Admiral Nimitz sending Shirley Temple out to fight the Japanese at Midway.

For Joan, it all started when she was twelve years old. The Archangel Michael, St. Catherine, and St. Margaret began to appear in her visions, telling her to drive the perfidious English (angels would use words like "perfidious") out of her country and make the Dauphin Charles king of all France. Pretty compelling stuff. So compelling that it only took hard-charging Joanie four short years to act on it.

In 1428, now sixteen, she eventually managed to be presented before Charles and convinced him of her vision. Not that it was a hard sell. The transcript of their meeting was probably something like this:

Joan: *I think you should be king.*
Charles: *Really?*
Joan: *So does the Archangel Michael.*
Charles: *That's really swell of him.*
Joan: *And I think we should wait for the Americans to help us.*
Charles: *Amer...icans. Sure. Why not?*
Joan: *So...*
Charles: *Yeah...*
Joan: *Great.*
Charles: *You bet ya.*

No doubt thrilled to actually have someone, anyone on his side, Charles got onboard the Joan of Arc bandwagon (once he realized that the Americans wouldn't be showing up for another 488 years) and sent her to help relieve the Siege of Orléans in May 1429. Since she was the closest thing to a Great French Commander that Charles's troops were ever going to see (and don't think they didn't know it), her mere presence on the battlefield was a great morale boost.

However, Joan's stay in the sun was fated to be brief, as it must always be for those who fight for France. Charles's main French rivals, the Burgundians, captured Joan on May 23, 1430, outside of the city of Compiègne. Instead of ransoming her back to Charles, she was sold off to the English for the considerable sum of ten thousand *livres*, which could buy you a demi-tasse of coffee in a snooty Parisian café.

In January 1431, she was put on trial for heresy in the French city of Rouen. To the English, it must have seemed obvious: a Frenchwoman who claimed to speak with angels and actually won on the battlefield. Surely, a deal with the devil had to be in the offing here! Of course, it was what we would today refer to as a kangaroo court; not sure what it would have been called back then, since kangaroos had not yet been discovered. Joan was accused of being a vicious killer, which was a hoot since she typically carried a banner and not a sword, despite her soldierly reputation. She was also accused of cross-dressing because of her military uniform.

She was found guilty of a laundry list of offenses: demonic visions, that cross-dressing thing, being against the Catholic Church, parking in a handicapped space, etc. Her tormentors, chief among whom was the swinish Bishop Cauchon, wanted her dead, but only a relapsed heretic could be executed. So in the next-to-last indignity they presented her with a situation where she had to choose between redonning her sinful male clothing or being raped, as female clothing offered no defense against groping prison guards. She chose the clothes and was burned at the stake (that was the last indignity, in case you were curious) on May 30, 1431—brave to the end.

After her boy Charles VII became king and recaptured Rouen, he made sure things were set straight. A retrial was held, and Joan was officially pronounced innocent in 1456. Unfortunately, she was still dead.

> "In certain public indecencies the difference between a dog and a Frenchman is not perceptible."

—Mark Twain

Joan sez: "God, I hate the French!"

15
BONUS: FROGLAND SECURITY THREAT LEVELS

LE SYSTÈME CONSULTATIF DE SÉCURITÉ POUR LA PATRIE

COLLABORATE
Severe Risk of Attack
Somebody Call The Americans

CAPITULATE
High Risk of Attack
Really No Point In Resisting

GROVEL
Significant Risk of Attack
Defeat All But Guaranteed

APPEASE
General Risk of Attack
Defeat A Near Certainty

COWER
Low Risk of Attack
Defeat A Distinct Possibility

> *"[The French] gibber like baboons even when you try to speak to them in their own wimpy language."*

—P. J. O'Rourke

16

RELIGIOUS WARS

Fight:	The Wars of Religion
Date:	1562 - 1598
Opponents:	French Catholics—House of Guise and the Catholic League
	versus
	French Huguenots (leave it to the Frogs to screw up spelling Protestant)—House of Bourbon and House of Valois (who were actually Catholic)
Incompetent French Leaders:	Among others, Henri of Navarre, Catherine de Medici, and Charles IX
Outcome:	French Win Some and They Lose Some

THE PATHETIC DETAILS:

This is a real confusing one with the only saving grace being that, since only the French got killed, it was a war everyone could get behind. It's also a useful history lesson to remember the next time some uppity Frog gets in your face about how intolerant Americans are. Just say, "Back off, Frenchy! At least I don't have to apologize for the St. Bartholomew's Day Massacre! Yeah, you heard me."

Anyway, to understand where all this hatred got started, no doubt you'll recall the old French saying *"Une foi, un loi, un roi."* You do remember that, right? Just in case you don't, it means "one faith, one law, one king." That pretty much bound the Catholic Church and the French monarchy together tightly. Anything else made you a heretic and a traitor, so it is understandable how many would view the entrance of Protestantism into France with a jaundiced eye.

As with just about every fight in Europe at this time, it started with a king dying prematurely. In this case, François II's untimely and, let's face it, just plain inconsiderate exit left his wife, Catherine de Medici, as regent for her ten-year-old son Charles IX. Though Catholic, Catherine worried for the safety of her son's regime against the powerful House of Guise, also Catholic. Catherine turned to the Huguenot House of Bourbon as a political counterweight. As a result, in January 1562 she backed the Edict of St. Germain that allowed for religious tolerance. In this case, Huguenots could worship openly outside of towns and privately within village limits. She might as well have put a KICK ME sign on the Protestants. Actually, a KILL ME sign would have been more apropos (notice how we snuck in a French word there?) as French Catholics intolerantly welcomed this Edict of Toleration with, how to put this delicately, a massacre at a Huguenot religious service in March 1562 in the town of Wassy.

This tiff at Wassy inaugurated an intermittent series of slaughters and campaigns that would consume the next thirty-six years. The most infamous atrocity was the St. Bartholomew's Day Massacre in August 1572

when Huguenots, in Paris for the marriage of Henri of Navarre, got a little more than they bargained for when Catholic mobs, not really considering what it would do to the tourism business, went on a three-day rampage that left three thousand dead, happily all of them French. Henri of Navarre was forced to convert to Catholicism at ~~rosary~~ sword point, though he reverted once he escaped the clutches of the House of Valois. (Typical politician: always flip-flopping.)

Charles did not live long after the massacre and was succeeded by his brother Henri III, noted for enjoying women's clothing (and to think that they burned poor ol' Joan of Arc for wearing *men's* clothing). The House of Valois was now hanging on by a thread. It was pretty much a given that no heir was about to spring forth from the loins of Henri III (or something like that), so all hopes were riding on the younger brother, François, Duke of Anjou, who had the bad grace to die in 1584. Henri III, last king of the Valois, Catholic, butcher of Huguenots, was to be succeeded by.... Henri of Navarre, House of Bourbon, Huguenot.

This all led to the amusingly named War of the Three Henries that pitted Henri III of Valois against Henri of Navarre (Bourbon) against Henri of Guise. While Henri of Guise was nominally an ally of Henri III, he was also the head of the Catholic League, which was a little too helpful in offering the Valois king advice on how to deal with those pesky Protestants, especially that rascally Henri of Navarre.

On Christmas Eve 1588, Henri of Valois invited Henri of Guise into his home at Blois for a strategy session. Unfortunately, for Guise, the only strategy good King Henri was interested in was killing his erstwhile partner. Guise's body was hacked to pieces, the remains burnt, the ashes cast to the wind. Now, it was the War of Two Henries, but the Catholic League didn't take Guise's murder too well and sent an army after Henri III. The last of the Valois line was forced to go, beret in hand, to his rival and future successor. It was now the War of the Two Allied Henries—one Catholic, the other Protestant—against the Enraged Catholics.

In July 1589, a monk put a knife into Henri III's belly as he sat on the commode, and now there was only one Henri, who the dying Henri summoned to his deathbed. Henri of Navarre emerged from that meeting as Henri IV, first king of the Bourbon dynasty.

Of course, Henri IV was still a Huguenot, even if he was the King of France, and he still had a Catholic League army in the field to contend with that now had the financial backing of Spain. Fighting would go on for nearly a decade longer, but in July 1593, Henri IV re-converted back to Catholicism. He is reputed to have said, *"Paris vaut bien une messe."* (Paris is well worth a Mass.) Henri IV may have sold out his Protestant base, but betrayal, cowardice, and cross-dressing are a way of life in La Belle France.

Henri did toss a bone to those he double-crossed in the form of the Edict of Nantes of 1598, which granted religious freedom to the Huguenots. That is, until it was revoked in 1685.

> *"He [Henri IV] was an immensely attractive figure both to women and to men—despite it being said that he was economic with bathing and smelled strongly of goat!"*
>
> —Alistair Horne, La Belle France, and you read that right. The man said a French king smelled like a goat.

17

TOY SOLDIERS

FRANCO-PRUSSIAN WAR TOY SOLDIER SET

$2.98

2 COMPLETE ARMIES
EVERY PIECE MOLDED ON ITS OWN BASE
RELIVE AGAIN THE FAMOUS BATTLES OF YESTERYEAR!
FORM YOUR OWN BATTLE LINES!
HOURS OF FUN
FOR THE WHOLE FAMILY!

Realistic battlefield diorama includes authentic French bistro complete with wait staff!

IMAGINARY WAR SCENE SHOWN

BATTLE OF SEDAN SET INCLUDES THE FOLLOWING:

FRENCH ARMY:
Emperor Napoléon III
150 high-ranking officers
150 court officials
100 infantrymen
50 cavalrymen
25 artillery pieces
500 prostitutes
976 white flags
All French pieces made from highest quality flexible plastic

PRUSSIAN ARMY:
10 infantrymen
2 cavalrymen
1 artillery piece
All Prussian pieces made from drop-forged steel

ORDER TODAY!

> "A fighting Frenchman runs away from even a she-goat."
>
> —Russian proverb

18
FAMOUS FRENCH FIGHTING SONGS

❝ "A Frenchman must be always talking, whether he knows anything of the matter or not." ❞

—Samuel Johnson, from Boswell's *Life of Johnson*

19

LE ROI SOLEIL

Name:	Louis XIV (The Sun King) (1638-1715)
Conflicts:	War of Devolution, Franco-Dutch War, War of the Reunions, Nine Years' War, and the War of the Spanish Succession
Opponents:	Pretty Much Everyone in Europe
Incompetent French Leader:	Louis XIV
Notable Catastrophe:	Louis XIV's reign

Nice legs, Louie.

(Louis XIV by Hyacinthe Rigaud)

THE DREARY DETAILS:

He became king when he was five years old. His birth came after twenty-three childless years for his parents, Louis XIII (not exactly noted for preferring the womenfolk, if you catch our drift, wink, wink) and Anne, who were so pleased that they christened their little bundle of joy Louis-Dieudonné (God-given). (With a nickname like that, are we surprised he had grand ideas?) His rule lasted for seventy-two years (fifty-four, if you count from when he actually had full control of the government). The state of Louisiana is named in his honor. He outlived all his children, and it was his great-grandson who succeeded him as Louis XV. And, not surprisingly, when a king lives that long, he makes a lot of trouble for everyone around him, especially when the king was as splashy and free-spending as Louis was.

Louis fought five major wars during his reign. With the largest army in Europe and the Holy Roman Empire distracted by an Ottoman invasion, Louis increased French territory at the expense of the Spanish and the Dutch. By French standards, it was the height of military glory; by Alexander the Great's standards, it was just another day's march. However, it all came at a terrible financial price, and tax rates on the already downtrodden peasants soared. Even Louis himself felt the pinch as he was forced to melt down the silver furniture from his sumptuous palace at Versailles to pay the bills for the Nine Years' War. The end of his reign was marked by the War of the Spanish Succession (see Chapter 21), which wrecked whatever remaining power the French military possessed.

On the domestic front, Louis reduced the authority of the nobility and clergy. (You don't think any of those powers went to the hoi polloi, do you?) He simultaneously diminished the role of the pope and increased the persecution of Huguenots (Protestants). He threw wild parties. As befits a

French monarch, he had more than his fair share of mistresses. National greatness (capturing Luxembourg and parts of Belgium?) came at the price of an absolute monarchy. Voltaire gushed that Louis's reign was an "eternally memorable age." The Duc de Saint-Simon observed, "There was nothing he liked so much as flattery, or, to put it more plainly, adulation…"

And, in the end, he left his country bankrupt. A lot of flash, but very little cash. How very French.

> "God seems to have forgotten all I have done for him."
>
> —Louis XIV

A FRENCH PRAYER

> "Our Father who art in Versailles, thy name is no longer hallowed; thy kingdom is diminished; thy will is no longer done on earth or on the waves. Give us our bread, which we totally lack...and deliver us from the Maintenon [Louis XIV's mistress]. Amen."

—French peasant adaptation of the Lord's Prayer

20

PARIS IS LOVELY THIS TIME OF YEAR

Folks have been loitering about the banks of the River Seine for a long time now. The first group that we know about was a tribe of Gauls that called themselves the Parisii, which some scholars say comes from a Gallic word that means "the working people." This is a big hint that the Gauls weren't French, lazy bastards that they are. The Romans eventually snagged the place in 52 B.C. and promptly named it Lutetia.

Around 310 A.D. during the short-lived reign of Julian the Apostate, Lutetia became the de facto capital of the beleaguered Western Roman Empire and was renamed Paris, which no doubt cost all the local businesses a fortune to redo their stationery. By the way, Julian the Apostate is a really cool name. Why don't we name our illustrious leaders this way anymore? Nancy the Annoying. Barney the Pederast. Barack the Purveyor of High Quality Health Insurance. Good times.

Where were we? Ah, yes. Paris.

So, in 508 A.D., Clovis the Frank, not to be confused with Clovis the Ambiguous, founder of the Merovingian dynasty, settled upon Paris as his capital city, and since that time, the City of Light has been a seat of commerce, government, culture, education, and self-absorbed, pompous, wine-guzzling buffoons. It has also played the part of turnstile to marauding armies rampaging back and forth across the countryside, with the invaders, more often than not, being the Frogs themselves.

CONFLICT	DATE	COMMENTARY
Viking Incursions	March 885	Paris is sacked by the Viking horde under Ragnar Lodbrok.
Hundred Years' War	May 1418	The Burgundian French under John the Fearless send the Dauphin scurrying to safety.
Hundred Years' War	December 1420	Under the terms of the Treaty of Troyes, the English King Henry V strolls right into Paris.
First Fronde	October 1648	The parliamentary faction seizes Paris during the First Fronde, sending Cardinal Mazarin, the child King Louis XIV and the rest of the royal faction fleeing for their lives.
French Revolution	July 1789	Angry Frogs seize the Bastille. Louis XVI loses control of Paris, followed in short order by the loss of his head.
Napoleonic Wars	March 1814	The Allies of the Sixth Coalition march into Paris and send Napoléon packing into his first exile.

Napoleonic Wars	March 1815	Napoléon returns! Louis XVIII abandons Paris without a shot fired.
Napoleonic Wars	June 1815	The War of the Seventh Coalition concludes with yet another army entering Paris without having to fight for it. Napoléon becomes the Emperor of the South Atlantic.
July Revolution (Second French Revolution)	July 1830	Sick of having a king, rampaging Parisians force the Bourbon King Charles X into exile and welcome Louis-Philippe, their new… king.
Revolution of 1848 (Third French Revolution)	February 1848	Rioting Parisians take over the city and chase the Orléanist King Louis Philippe into exile. Second Republic is born. Louis-Napoléon Bonaparte lurks in the wings.
Franco-Prussian War	January 1871	Reduced to eating horses, rats and even elephants, Paris surrenders to Kaiser Wilhelm I, ending the Franco-Prussian War.
Paris Commune (Fourth French Revolution)	March 1871	Angry about losing to the Prussians, French Communards seize Paris from other Frenchmen.
Paris Commune	May 1871	The Third Republic Strikes Back! The French Army launches Bloody Week and takes Paris back from the Commune.

World War II	June 1940	Nazis steamroll the Frogs. The subsequent actions of the Vichy makes some think that they really wanted to be on the German side all along.
World War II	August 1944	Allies liberate the City of Light. Everyone pretends the French actually helped.
Student Uprisings	May 1968	As a result of widespread strikes and student protests, Charles de Gaulle is forced to flee Paris for a French military headquarters in Germany.

❝ *Vegas didn't lose a single inch of ground to the Nazi war machine.* ❞

—Reason #4 from Late Night with David Letterman's "Top Ten Ways Las Vegas is Better than Paris"

21

THE SPANISH SUCCESSION DOES NOT SUCCEED

Fight:	War of the Spanish Succession
Date:	1701-1714
Opponents:	France
	Bavaria
	Spain versus
	English
	Dutch
	Prussians
	Austrians
Incompetent French Leader:	Camille de Tallard
Outcome:	Louis XIV's delusion dream of dominating Europe comes to a crashing end

THE PATHETIC DETAILS:

It's one of the most important wars no one's ever heard of. Despite a series of expensive conflicts that really netted little for all the trouble, at the end of the seventeenth century, France still fielded the largest army (some historians invariably add "most powerful," but who are they kidding? If the French Army was that *puissant*, they would have steamrolled through the Netherlands, and France's eastern border today would rest on the Vistula) and largest population in Europe. The Thirty Years' War had devastated nearly every state on the Continent, especially the German ones, the English were preoccupied with Ireland, and as the French had avoided the worst of the fighting, they were almost, by default, the biggest kid on the block.

Given the name of the war, it should come as no great surprise that it all centered on the Spanish throne. Fights over succession rights were nothing new to Europe and typically happened when a king died unexpectedly before siring an heir. However, in this instance, Charles II, only surviving son of Philip IV, was still very much alive, but had been born unsound of mind and body. His case of the infamous Hapsburg Lip (mandibular prognathism) was so pronounced that it was said that he couldn't chew his own food without assistance. (All that royal inbreeding finally catches up with you, ya know?) There would be no successor; he would be the last of the Spanish Hapsburg monarchs.

At stake, once Charles died, was not just Spain itself, but all her holdings in Italy, the Netherlands, the Philippines, and the Americas. The Austrian Hapsburgs (Leopold I was the husband of Philip IV's younger daughter) and the French Bourbons (Louis XIV had landed Philip IV's eldest daughter) maneuvered to gain this choice plum and win an empire on the cheap.

However, no one was really excited about yet another war (even kings occasionally grow weary of seeing their treasuries bankrupted and their subjects slaughtered), so a compromise candidate was found (five-year-old Joseph Ferdinand of the Bavarian Wittelsbach family), but he had the bad manners to die of smallpox in 1699. And you thought kids today with their noses glued to their electronic gizmos were jerks; at least, they don't go around dying for no good reason just when you need them. Of course, if you asked them to mow the yard or something, they might just up and keel over on you. Kids.

Anyway, Europe was right back to where it had started, and Charles II wasn't getting any younger (or smarter, for that matter). Charles himself, undoubtedly nudged in the right direction by pro-French advisors, finally decided that Philip, Duke of Anjou, 2nd son of Louis XIV's only legitimate surviving son (Louis the Grand ~~Dolphin~~ Dauphin) should succeed him and gain all of Spain and its empire (nothing to add, but it just seemed like we'd gone a few sentences without a parenthetical thought).

The rest of Europe was appalled, but, when Charles II finally did die on November 1, 1700, and Louis's grandson became Philip V, king of Spain, the English and Dutch reluctantly accepted it as a *fait accompli* (French for "it's a done deal"). Louis, on the other hand, not knowing a good "done" deal when he saw it, grabbed Spanish forts in the Netherlands and cut off the English and Dutch from trading with Spain.

On September 7, 1701, a grand alliance was formed between Austria, England, the United Provinces (Dutch), Prussia, and most of the German states to take on the French-Spanish Bourbon monstrosity.

For the next thirteen years, war raged across Spain, Italy, the Netherlands, and Germany. In the end, Philip V got to keep his crown, but was forced to give up any notions of succeeding his grandfather; Spain and France would never be united under one Bourbon king. To add insult to injury, King Phil also now presided over a much diminished empire, as the war cost him the Spanish Netherlands, Italy, Sicily, and Gibraltar. France itself lost very little territory, but Louis's dream of dominating Europe was *finis*. The Revolution was one step closer.

Notable Catastrophe: Battle of Blenheim

Edward Creasy included Blenheim in his famous *Fifteen Decisive Battles of the World* and observed "had it not been for Blenheim, all Europe might at this day suffer under the effect of French conquests resembling those of Alexander in extent and those of the Romans in durability." Thank God that didn't happen. Europeans are insufferable enough without all of them resembling the French.

It was the summer of 1704, and a combined Franco-Bavarian army commanded by Camille d'Hostun de la Baume, Duc de Tallard, and the Bavarian Elector Maximilian II Emanuel was driving on Vienna. Through a series of brilliant maneuvers, Anglo-Dutch forces led by John Churchill, Duke of Marlborough, left the Netherlands and joined the Austrian Army led by Prince Eugene of Savoy in the Bavarian countryside. Marlborough (whose descendants include the late lamented Winston Churchill and the late unlamented Princess Diana) was probably the foremost military strategist of his time. Creasy noted that Marlborough "never fought a battle he did not win and never besieged a place that he did not take." All in all, it spelled bad news for the Frogs.

Marlborough, now, blocked the French path to Vienna, though his army was slightly outnumbered (sixty thousand versus fifty-six thousand), but he was still not out of the woods. If he did nothing, the French Army in Italy under Villeroi could march north to join Tallard and the Elector. If he attacked immediately, the numbers did not favor him, and a defeat could reopen the door to Vienna and remove Austria from the war. In true stiff upper lip British fashion, Marlborough went on the offensive.

What ensued on the afternoon of August 13, 1704, was a rout of epic proportions. After hours of bloody fighting, Marlborough's division on the left and Eugene's on the right were able to roll up both French flanks.

Tallard was captured, and his army suffered twelve thousand dead, another fourteen thousand captured, and the loss of all its artillery. Bavaria surrendered and was lost as an ally to France. The war would drag on for another ten years, but the French would remain firmly on the defensive. Louis's window to dominate Europe had just slammed shut (or is that a door? Mustn't mix metaphors.).

> "Things went from bad to worse until just about anybody could defeat the French. On one occasion, Louis's favorite regiment was knocked out by a man named Lumley."

—Will Cuppy, *The Decline and Fall of Practically Everybody*

22

FRENCH ARMY PHYSICAL FITNESS TEST

Let's face it. Military life can be grueling. There are a lot of physical demands placed on soldiers and sailors. Long hikes, lack of sleep, working in hot weather, crappy food, working in cold weather, avoiding the Shore Patrol, chasing down hookers. Not just any lard-butt has what it takes to be in the military, especially the French Army.

Not surprisingly, every military in the world that's worth its salt tests its service members periodically to see if they're within standards.

For example, the U.S. Marine Corps Physical Fitness Test consists of the following:

1. Pull-ups

2. Sit-ups (Two minutes)

3. Three-mile run

Additionally, there is the Combat Fitness Test with three more events:

1. 880-yard "Movement to Contact" in boots and combat utility pants ("boots and utes")

2. Thirty-pound overhead ammo can lift (Two minutes)

3. "Maneuver under Fire"

    a. Twenty-five yard crawl

    b. Drag a simulated casualty for ten yards

    c. Carry a simulated casualty for sixty-five yards

    d. Carry two thirty-pound ammo cans for seventy-five yards

    e. Grenade toss into marked circle 22.5 yards away

    f. Three pushups

    g. Ammo can sprint to finish line

Nothing terribly complicated.
Let's see what the French Army requires…
1. Blood alcohol test (must be greater than .08)

2. Arm raises (must be able to maintain this for four hours)

3. 500-yard panicked dash

4. 250-yard belly grovel

5. Four-mile mass retreat (entire unit must participate)

Who knew it was so physically demanding, being in the French Army?

> *"The French do not live on happiness."*

—Andre Maurois

23

NEW FRANCE NO MORE

Fight: French and Indian War
Date: 1754-1763
Opponents: France
Indians (Native Americans, if you're a PC weenie)
versus
Great Britain
American Colonies
Incompetent French Leader: Louis-Joseph de Montcalm, among many, many others
Outcome: Crushing French defeat with the loss of virtually all of North American possessions. French give up on hockey. Indians investigate the benefits of casinos and bingo halls.

EMBARRASSING AMERICAN FACT:

Lieutenant Colonel George Washington, mature beyond his twenty-two years of age, was surrounded by a French force at Fort Necessity in Pennsylvania and compelled to surrender on July 3, 1754. Ouch!

THE PATHETIC DETAILS:

The French and British had been scrapping over North America ever since both sides could muster up enough strength to fend off marauding Indians, ever-present famine, and coyotes (that doesn't seem right). Maybe not coyotes, but tomahawk-wielding Mohicans and starvation kept colonists busy for quite some time, but eventually, the French in New France (modern-day Canada) and the British with its colonies on the eastern seaboard of the Atlantic got around to duking it out. The Indians, stuck in the middle, usually chose the French as allies since drunks tend to gravitate toward each other. Now, most astute humans (i.e., anyone with an IQ over fourteen) are astounded that anyone would ever willingly side with the French. (For the record, we would side with flesh-eating space aliens intent on destroying the human race before we allied with the French.) However, we believe that the Indian decision was the correct one for the following reasons:

1. British victory would lead to the creation of the United States. (Trust us, the Indians saw this all very clearly. They're also masters at picking winning lottery numbers.)

2. Formation of the United States would lead to expansion all the way to the Pacific Ocean and displacement of all Indian tribes.

3. Therefore, the British had to be stopped at all cost.

4. In the event of a French victory, Indians would then turn on their erstwhile allies and march (canoe?) on Paris because everyone beats the French.

Unfortunately, they did not know Rule #1 of Being a Great Indian Commander: Never ally with the French. An alternate explanation is that they knew, but forgot after an epic all-night bender.

There had been several other conflicts before the big blowup in 1754 with forgettable names like: King William's War, Queen Anne's War, (the strangely overlooked) Queen Latifah's War, and King George's War. The War of Jenkins' Ear was probably in there somewhere, but we slept through that lecture. Anyway, all of those scrapes were sideshows to the main events going on in Europe. The French and Indian War was the exact opposite; it started here and spread to Europe two years later (where it is called the Seven Years' War).

As American colonists continued to push west, conflict with both the French and Indians was probably inevitable. On May 28, 1754, a small party of Virginia militia, under the command of George Washington (THE George Washington), fought a skirmish with an equally small party of French Canadian militia in the Ohio Country near what is today Uniontown, Pennsylvania. Then, it was off to the races, though neither side could support the sort of large armies that would routinely trample Europe underfoot.

The French had some successes, such as the defeat of Braddock's Expedition at the Battle of Monongahela in July 1755 and the capture of Fort William Henry in August 1757 (the battle and resulting slaughter of British prisoners by France's Indian allies was grist for James Fennimore Cooper's novel *Last of the Mohicans*.). However, the French being French (drunk, indecisive, undisciplined) and the Indians being Indians (drunk, decisive, undisciplined) were finally defeated by the combined weight of professional British arms and swarms of American militia.

Though France was driven off the North American mainland completely, it was allowed to retain two tiny islands off Newfoundland and some other islands in the Caribbean.

New France was dead. *Vive Nouveau France!*

Notable Catastrophe: Battle of the Plains of Abraham

It was September 13, 1759. British forces had kept Quebec City, the capital of New France, under a loose siege for three months. The French forces inside, led by General Montcalm, outnumbered their British counterparts by almost three to one (roughly fifteen thousand to five thousand troops), but most of them were green militiamen. General James Wolfe's British troops were experienced regulars. Of course, with the French, be it seasoned veteran or raw recruit, humiliating disaster is just a day's march away.

On that morning, Wolfe assembled his entire army on the Plains of Abraham just outside the city and offered battle. Probably fearing that the British deployment was a feint, Montcalm accepted but brought less than half of his army to bear.

It was all over in less than an hour. British discipline shattered a series of ill-advised French charges. Routed, the French hightailed it back to Quebec City. Both Wolfe and Montcalm were mortally wounded and would not see the next morning. Quebec City would surrender five days later. Montreal would be captured in 1760.

France would never know the joys of professional hockey.

"You play with them. This game is too rough."

> "Only thing worse than a Frenchman is a Frenchman who lives in Canada."
>
> —Ted Nugent, sage, savant, scholar

24
WHAT'S WRONG WITH THIS PICTURE?

Kids, name all the mistakes this French soldier is making while fleeing for his life!

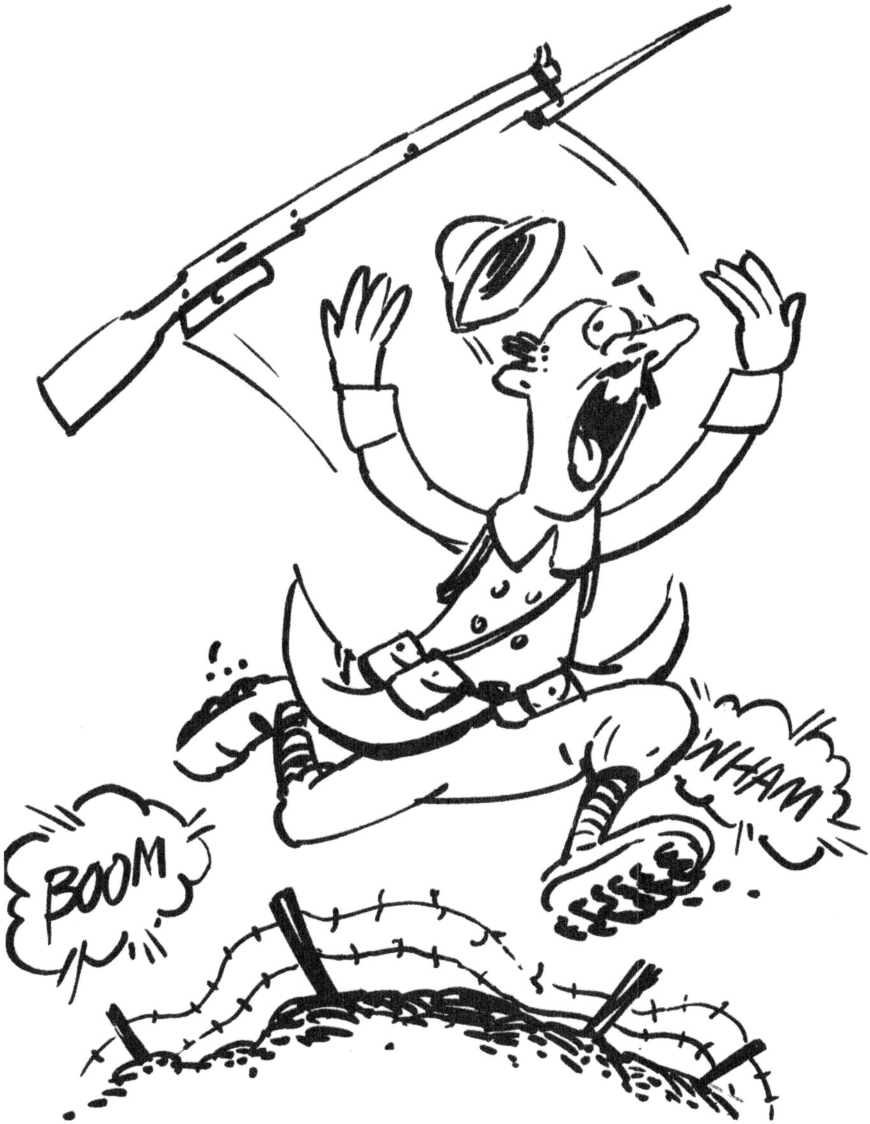
BOOM
WHAM

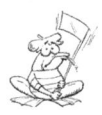

1. Drop the rifle, man. For God's sake, it only slows you down.

2. Drop the pack, man. For God's sake, it only slows you down.

3. Where are his comrades? As we all know, the French soldier never flees except in a panic stricken mob.

4. Beret? Where's the beret? That almost looks like a military helmet!

25
TOOLS OF THE TRADE — EQUIPMENT FOR THE POILU

- Running shoes

- Bulletproof vest (backplate only)

- German dictionary

- White cloth (great for picnics and surrenders)

- Wine opener

- (Cheese) knife

- Crackers (to cleanse the palate)

- Michelin Guide (even in retreat, one can find the most *merveilleux* places to dine)

- Rifle (optional)

Weight saving tips (leave the following behind to lighten that load)
- Toothpaste
- Soap
- Deodorant
- Ammunition
- Rifle

> "Bonjour! You cheese-eating surrender monkeys!"
>
> —Groundskeeper Willie, *The Simpsons*

26
A MOVEABLE FEAST

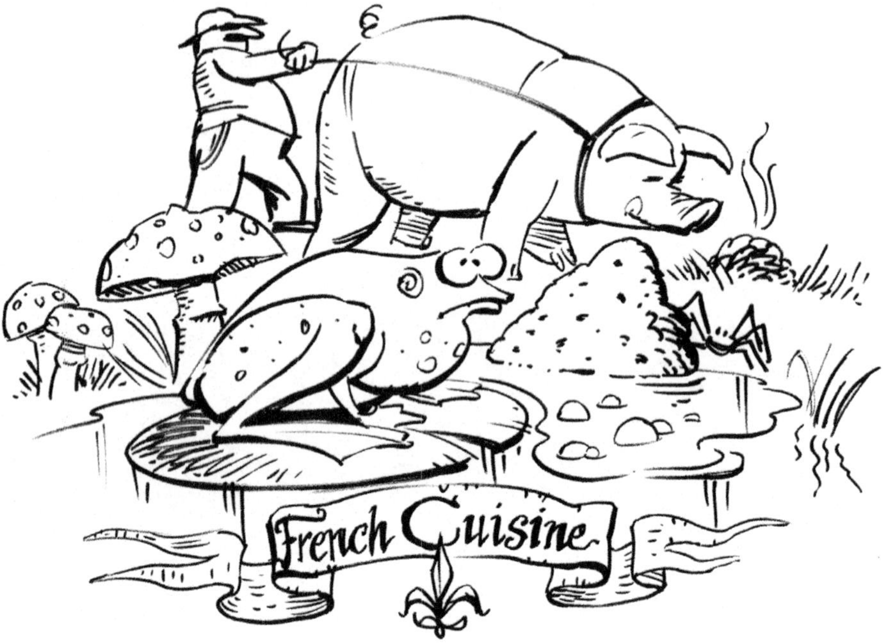
French Cuisine

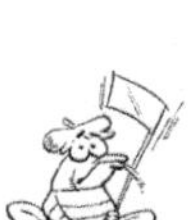

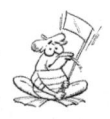

> *"How do they expect a one-party system in a country which has over 246 different kinds of cheese?"*

——Charles de Gaulle

27

THE ONE TIME THE FROGS CAME THROUGH

Name: *Comte* François Joseph Paul de Grasse (1722-1788)
Conflict: American Revolutionary War
Opponent: British Royal Navy

THE NOT SO DREARY DETAILS:

The United States Navy doesn't make a habit of naming its ships after dirty, good-fer-nothing, low-down furriners, especially Frogs. So, when it really does happen, you know it's got to be a big deal. USS *Comte de Grasse* (DD-974) of the *Spruance*-class served proudly from 1978 until her decommissioning in 1998. There is no truth to the rumor that the destroyer was ceremonially surrendered.

The man behind the name was the son of an ancient noble family from southern France. The Count started his naval career with the Knights of Malta at the tender age of twelve. During the War of the Austrian

Succession, de Grasse was captured after the disastrous French naval defeat (talk about a string of redundancies) at the First Battle of Finisterre in 1747.

In the intervening years, he made steady progress through the ranks, and, by the time the French entered the American Revolutionary War, he was a commodore. He had participated in several inconclusive duels with the British at Ushant and in the Caribbean when destiny tapped him on the shoulder.

In August 1781, de Grasse, now a rear admiral, received an urgent plea from General George Washington for naval assistance. With Lord Cornwallis's beleaguered force trapped between Nathanael Greene's army coming up from the Carolinas and Washington's moving south from New York, the American commander wanted to ensure that the British couldn't escape by sea. The surrender of a second major British army (Burgoyne's at Saratoga being the first) would probably convince George III that the American colonists could not be defeated.

But before all that could happen, the French Navy would have to hold its own against a Royal Navy that made up for numerical and technological inferiority with aggressiveness, superb seamanship, and the fact that its sailors and officers were not French.

De Grasse left the Caribbean and arrived off the coast of Virginia on August 30, 1781. The British fleet was nowhere to be found, but, once it was realized that Cornwallis was cornered like a rat, albeit a well-dressed one, in Yorktown, Admiral Thomas Graves sailed to the rescue from New York City.

Outnumbering Graves by twenty-four to nineteen ships of the line, de Grasse put to sea on September 5 and, over the next five days, fought the British to a standstill in a series of rather uninspiring engagements collectively known to us as the Second Battle of the Virginia Capes. Having had the worst of it, Graves gave up and sailed for home. Cornwallis was doomed and surrendered a month later. *Comte* de Grasse and the French Navy had done just enough.

Unfortunately for the good Count, this crucial, if dull, victory was the high point of his career. The British would have their revenge in less than a year. On April 12, 1782, between the islands of Dominica and Guadeloupe, de Grasse's fleet was thoroughly whipped by Admiral George Rodney at the Battle of the Saints. De Grasse was captured aboard his flagship *Ville de Paris* (everyone gets to capture Paris, it seems). Once he was released, he probably wished he had stayed with the British as a court of inquiry blamed him for the Saints defeat.

As a final note, his five children fled France during the French Revolution and came to the United States.

Merci, Comte de Grasse.

> "The Almighty in His infinite wisdom did not see fit to create Frenchmen in the image of Englishmen."

——Winston Churchill

20

MYTH BUSTER #2

MYTH: Without the French, the Patriots could never have defeated the British during the Revolution, and there would not be a United States of America today.

TRUTH: It's gotten to the point where you can't even look at a French flag cross-eyed without some dewy-eyed, sophisticated she-male saying, "Without the French, the Patriots could never have defeated the British during the Revolution, and there would not be a United States of America today." Oh, brother.

We see right through this subterfuge. Us bailing them out in two world wars is only just payment for them bailing us out back in 1776.

Let me tell you, sister, that ain't the way it was.

If you attended an American public school (even if you actually decided to take American "history" as your elective instead of Digital Photography or Floral Arrangements or Oppressed Minority Liberation Theory), here's a timeline for you that might prove illuminating:

Battle of Lexington & Concord—April 19, 1775
Declaration of American Independence—July 4, 1776
France and United States enter into alliance—February 6, 1778
France declares war on Great Britain—June 17, 1778

While our Froggish friends waited to see if we Americans could actually make a fight of it (which was absolutely their right; after all, we sat out both world wars for several years, improbably hoping they'd all just kill themselves off and go away), here are some of the "minor events" that happened before the French joined the fun:

EVENT	DATE	AMERICAN TROOPS PRESENT	FRENCH TROOPS PRESENT
Battle of Bunker Hill	16 June 1775	2,400	0
Battle of Long Island	27 August 1776	10,000	0
Battle of Trenton	26 December 1776	2,400	0
Battle of Princeton	3 January 1777	4,500	0
Winter Encampment at Morristown	January 1777 to May 1777	8,300	0
Battle of Oriskany	6 August 1777	800	0
Battle of Bennington	16 August 1777	2,350	0
Battle of Brandywine	11 September 1777	14,600	0

Battle of Germantown	4 October 1777	11,000	0
Battle of Saratoga	10 October 1777	6,600	0
Winter Encampment at Valley Forge	December 1777 to June 1778	12,000	0

All of that and nary a Frenchman to be seen (or smelt). Only after the French thought the water was safe did they jump in. For all of you "French help in 1776 = American help in 1944" whiners, this would be the equivalent of waiting for the Russians to cross the Rhine into the Alsace-Lorraine before launching the Normandy invasion.

All right, so now the Frogs are in the game. They provide arms and money, but let's have a look at the actual heavy-lifting of combat after the French entry into the war.

EVENT	DATE	AMERICAN TROOPS PRESENT	FRENCH TROOPS PRESENT	COMMENTARY
Battle of Monmouth	28 June 1778	11,000	0	Last major battle between the main Patriot and British armies. No French in the area.
First Battle of Savannah	29 December 1778	850	0	British turn their attention south and capture this important Georgia port. No Frogs spotted.

Battle of Vincennes	23-25 February 1779	172	0	Patriot victory in the wilds of Indiana untainted by the odiferous presence of the French.
Second Battle of Savannah	16 September – 20 October 1779	2,000	3,500	French participation ends in disaster as *Comte* d'Estaing sails off into the sunset, which is kind of hard to do in the western Atlantic
Siege of Charleston	April – May 1780	5,500	0	Enough of a catastrophe without needing a Frenchman to ruin it further. Entire American force surrenders.
Battle of Camden	16 August 1780	3,700	0	Another major disaster for the Patriots.
Battle of King's Mountain	7 October 1780	900	0	Patriot militia wipes out Loyalist militia without any assistance from the Frogs whatsoever.

Battle of Cowpens	17 January 1781	1,900	0	While Cowpens is the basis for the final battle in the dreadful Mel Gibson movie *The Patriot*, there were no French present to sully this tremendous American victory
Battle of Guilford Court House	15 March 1781	4,400	0	Nathanael Greene loses the battle, but helps win the war. That's how you know the French weren't involved.
Siege of Yorktown	September – October 1781	11,100	7,800	And now the Frogs show up! At least they made it count.

Men like the *Marquis* de Lafayette served honorably in the American cause, but Lafayette arrived in America against the wishes of his king prior to France's official entry into the war and only commanded American troops. *Comte* de Rochambeau, who joined Washington in dealing the final blow to Cornwallis at Yorktown, actually spent the prior year idling about Newport, Rhode Island in support of a French squadron trapped in Narragansett Bay by the Brits.

So, let us make it clear: the French did provide assistance, especially financial, but, for the most part, it was an attempt to win back territory from a distracted British Empire in India and the Caribbean. In the end, as always, the hard work was done by Americans.

> "France looks great and seems swell, but it acts hideously. It's the Ted Bundy [noted American serial killer] of European nations."
>
> —Dennis Boyles, *Vile France*

29

"KNOCK, KNOCK. WHO'S THERE? I GIVE UP!" THE FINE ART OF SURRENDERING

It's inevitable. At some point, the French soldier, be it the lowliest private or loftiest general, will have to surrender. Human flesh can only take so much, and, once the baguettes, Chardonnay, and *pâte de foie gras* are exhausted, what can be done? *Mon Dieu*! A man can hardly be expected to throw his life away when all he has to resist is his rifle, several hundred rounds of ammunition, three hand grenades, four days of emergency rations, a fortified position, and an intact chain of command. *Non*! You ask too much. Let the idiot Americans throw their lives away defending their McDonald's and Disneyworld, their families and homes, and Paris. And how long can a man possibly run? It's the fourth day of the war, and we have been fleeing for 3 ½ days.

As everyone knows, the moment of surrender is the most dangerous time on the battlefield. The capturing soldiers in their anger or fear or confusion might mistake the surrendering foe for something dangerous like a fanatical Japanese samurai or a determined American Marine or an enraged elk. No, it's imperative that one conveys the proper message. A message that says, "I'm not fighting. I'm not a threat. I'm French."

Here are a few tips to help the surrender process:

1. A thoughtful letter before hostilities break out announcing your intention to capitulate is a welcome gesture sure to be appreciated by whatever army is about to defeat you.

2. White wine, white flag. Savor the symmetry.

3. Pre-translated military secrets ready to hand over are a great way to break the ice.

4. Don't wait for them to ask you to point out the Jews and other undesirables in your unit. Show some initiative, man!

5. Nothing says "I give up!" like a rousing rendition of *Deutschland Über Alles*. Bonus points if you know all the words to the *Horst Wessel Lied*.

6. Don't let your captors risk their health on skanky prostitutes. Not when you've got a perfectly good sister at home.

7. Disarming you will only cost your enemy valuable time on his drive to capture Paris. Be considerate. Throw away all of your weapons before you throw in the towel.

8. Keep those hands high! Surrender like you really mean it. Everyone hates a half-assed quitter.

9. Be in the first hundred to call it quits, and you could get a bottom bunk in Building 4, Block C at Stalag 3 near Augsburg. It's considered the Club Med of the German POW camp system.

10. Remember that confinement isn't forever. Those idiot Americans will eventually stop their incompetent dithering and win the war.

> "They wanted all the French to be free and equal and happy, and they tried to bring this about by decapitating as many of them as possible."
>
> —Will Cuppy, *The Decline and Fall of Practically Everybody*

"We must be careful the revolution does not cause a brain drain."

30

BUT I AM NAPOLÉON! NO. REALLY.
HE WAS.

Name: Napoléon Bonaparte
Conflicts: French Revolutionary War, Napoleonic Wars
Opponents: Pretty Much Everyone in Europe (yet again)

The Young, Hip Napoléon

(*Bonaparte on the Bridge at Arcole* by Antoine-Jean Gros)

THE MAN:

He was born on August 15, 1769, in the town of Ajaccio on the island of Corsica into a family of minor Corsican nobility and Italian descent. When he was accepted into a French military school at ten years of age, he had to learn to speak French. He was teased by the boys in school for his marked Italian accent, which stayed with him his entire life. He would rocket to prominence during the French Revolution, and from there, his rare mix of ambition and ability and good timing took him to the very apex of world power. His name was Napoleone Buonoparte, later modified to the more French-sounding Napoléon Bonaparte, and still later, simply, Napoléon I, Emperor of France.

Napoleonic Myth: Napoléon was about 5'7" tall, which made him about average height for the early nineteenth century. British wartime propaganda and some confusion between the English inch and the French *pouce* as units of measurement contributed to the widespread belief that Nappy was some kind of circus midget. Compounding this problem even further, his nickname *Le Petit Corporal* has been misinterpreted over the years as a reference to the Emperor's height and not as a term of affection.

Career: Bonaparte came to prominence during the turmoil of the French Revolution. His first military triumph drove the British fleet from the vital port of Toulon, which had revolted against the Revolution. How revolting! His masterful performance, coupled with some shrewd political schmoozing, earned him a promotion to brigadier general. A year later, in Paris, in October 1795, he dispersed another revolt that was threatening the National Convention with the famed "whiff of grapeshot."

With most of France's professional military leadership too well acquainted with the guillotine or taking the hint and skedaddling before assuming a headless posture, Bonaparte's skill and energy and (most importantly) victories brought him instant prestige. He also managed to hook up with the alluring and not-exactly-hard-to-hook-up-with Joséphine de Beauharnais at this time, as she was conveniently available since her inconveniently unavailable husband General Alexandre de Beauharnais had parted company from his skull in 1794.

Bonaparte, then, turned his attentions to Italy, where, in the campaign of 1796-97, he beat the daylights out of the armies of Austria and the Papal States. He used these famous victories to increase his political leverage back in France.

Not content with European victories, he next suggested a trip to Egypt. A little tourism. A little grab a colony here. A little annoy the British there. The Directory was more than happy to get this ambitious, talented, and dangerous man away, far away. Unfortunately, for the would-be conqueror, the British did more than just get annoyed. Despite finding the Rosetta Stone and the Sphinx, defeating a Mameluke horde at the Battle of the Pyramids, and beating up on various Ottoman armies, it was all for naught when Lord Nelson's fleet sailed into Aboukir Bay and literally wiped out the French squadron on August 1, 1798, at the incorrectly named Battle of the Nile. No navy, no overseas triumphs. It would be a lesson that Napoléon would learn (actually, not learn) continually over the next seventeen years.

After an ultimately unsuccessful foray into Syria, Napoléon left his army to its fate and bugged out of Egypt on August 24, 1799. Some claim the Directory had recalled him; others insist that he knew the gig was up and got out while the Royal Navy had left him the opportunity. Regardless, he returned to France with his lustre undiminished and joined a plot to seize power in the coup of 18 Brumaire (the Revolutionary Frogs were so darn revolutionary, they even changed the calendar), which is November 9 to the rest of us. He was quickly appointed First Consul.

After a brief campaign to grab Italy back from the Austrians, punctuated by the epic victory at Marengo, a relative calm settled over Europe. First Consul Bonaparte sent troops to restore French control over Haiti, but, after seeing his army wiped out by yellow fever and local resistance, he decided to get out of the Western Hemisphere and sold all of France's remaining North American possessions to the United States in the controversial Louisiana Purchase.

His previous appointment as Consul for Life in May 1802 proving unfulfilling (and, after all, who would want to spend the rest of his life as a mere consul; it's humiliating when you think about it), he went for it all and crowned himself Emperor on December 2, 1804. No one else was amused, and war seemed an appropriate response.

The next ten years would see Napoléon and his enemies fight over just about every square foot of Europe—from Spain to Russia. His greatest victories included Austerlitz (December 1805), Jena (October 1806), and Wagram (July 1809). When the odds were even, he was almost unbeatable. However, his invasion of Russia proved disastrous (see below), and eventually his empire was faced with the coalition of Britain, Spain, Russia, Portugal (really?), Prussia, Sweden, and Austria. Man, when the Portuguese are against you, you know all is lost. I mean that's like having the dude who runs the local crystal meth lab turn you into the cops for an outstanding warrant. Not that that has ever happened to the author…

Rising to the challenge, Napoléon was at his most brilliant in the retreat of 1813, but even his genius could not fend off such long odds. The Sixth Coalition dealt Boney a crushing defeat at the Battle of Leipzig in

October 1813 from which he was unable to recover. The Allies captured Paris on March 31, 1814, and Napoléon abdicated on April 11. He was exiled to the island of Elba off the coast of Italy. It was a pleasant place, but Napoléon wasn't exactly the retiring sort. He checked out on February 26, 1815, and made a beeline for France, intending to crash the Bourbon King Louis XVIII's party.

Perhaps not understanding what the Duke of Wellington meant about Nappy's mere presence being worth about thirty-five thousand men on the battlefield (some attribute this saying to the Prussian Field Marshal Blücher), Louis sent a single regiment to stop him. It didn't work, and the French people, nostalgic for defeat and deprivation, welcomed back their emperor

Demonstrating his incredible energy and organizational skills yet again, Napoléon quickly raised a regular army of nearly two hundred thousand men. He would need that army because the Austrians, British, Prussians, and Russians weren't interested in seeing Napoléon the First *Part Deux*.

The emperor had to act fast before the Allies could consolidate their widely dispersed forces. His plan was audacious: with his new army, he would march into Belgium and strike the scattered English, Dutch, and Prussian forces before the Austrians and Russians could arrive. However, Napoléon's own personal brand of magic, now badly faded, required capable subordinates, and his marshals, grown soft with royal titles and hot babes, failed him badly. Missing an opportunity to defeat the British and Prussians in detail at Quatre Bras and Ligny respectively, Napoléon was finally forced to attack the Duke of Wellington's strong defensive position near the village of Waterloo on June 18, 1815. It was a near thing, but the arrival of Blücher's Prussians turned the tide in favor of the Allies. Napoléon lost half of his army in the rout. He abdicated for the second and final time on June 22. The Hundred Days were over.

Since Napoléon didn't seem to take to the nice-guy Club Med approach, the British carefully prepared his travel arrangements this second go-round. They shipped him off to the island of Saint Helena in the middle of the South Atlantic, where he remained until his death on May 5, 1821.

Vive l'Empereur.

NOTABLE CATASTROPHE:

Obviously, it wasn't all wine and roses for the great Napoléon since he ended up on a rock in the Atlantic Ocean feeding seagulls, while his lesser gifted opponents all wound up as dukes and counts and earls and got lots of chicks.

Given the scope of his empire, many French defeats were out of his control. The decisive naval defeat at Trafalgar (October 21, 1805) and the dismal and brutal Peninsular War in Spain (1808-1814), for example, took place beyond his direct command.

The doozy that can be laid entirely at his doorstep is the invasion of Russia. By 1811, Russia was the only power on the Continent that stood beyond Napoléon's control. Austria and Prussia had surrendered. Spain was occupied, though a vicious guerilla war was in progress. England could not be conquered, but did not have the land strength to contest Napoléon without aid from others. That left Russia.

After the Peace of Tilsit was signed in 1807, the Continent was nominally at peace. However, the price Russia paid for peace with France was adhering to the Bonapartist "Continental System," which prohibited trade with Great Britain. Being a Great Power in its own right, Russia resented being told who they could trade with. Napoléon, in turn, resented the Russian resentment. Both sides massed armies for the fight to come.

Napoléon, being Napoléon, got the first blow in and invaded Russia on June 23, 1812. The Russians lost battle after battle to *La Grande Armée*, which started the campaign at nearly seven hundred thousand strong. Thereafter, the Russians retreated, destroying everything it left behind. This scorched-earth strategy angered the armchair Russian nobility sitting safely back in Moscow, who did not actually have to face the Corsican ogre on the battlefield. General Barclay de Tolly was sacked. The aged General Kutuzov took over, looked at the situation calmly, and… kept retreating.

However, he was eventually forced to confront Napoléon at the Battle of Borodino on September 7, 1812. It was the bloodiest fight of the Napoleonic Wars with combined casualties somewhere between seventy thousand to one hundred thousand dead and wounded. Kutuzov probably gave the Tsar a big "I told you so" and resumed the retreat. The French entered Moscow a few days later.

Now, here is where it gets stupid. According to the traditions of the day, when you captured the enemy's capital, they were supposed to surrender or, at least, enter into negotiations. The Russians had no intention of doing that. Of course, one problem was the capital of Russia was actually St. Petersburg, but the maps back then weren't as good as the ones we have today, and Peter the Great may not have sent out any courtesy "I moved my capital city" cards back in 1703 when he left Moscow.

Nevertheless, Napoléon had a huge problem. The Russians weren't quitting. They had a huge pool of manpower to replenish their army from. There were no supplies to be found, and Moscow started burning on September 14, and the fire lasted for four days. After thirty-six days, Napoléon eventually got the hint and decided it was time to head back home.

But going home wasn't going to be easy. Smart Russian maneuvering and French dithering forced the Frogs to use the same devastated route back that they had used coming in. There would be no living off the land, and, if Napoléon (and post-Revolution French armies in general) had one weakness, it was that he never paid a great deal of attention to his logistics. Hungry and harassed by Cossacks, things went from bad to worse as the Russian winter closed in. Starvation, frostbite, exhaustion. It was one of the greatest nightmares in military history.

For Napoléon, though, there was one final insult to be added to the injury. At the beginning of December, he learned of a possible uprising against his rule back in Paris (the Malet coup d'état). In a reprise of his Egyptian adventure, he abandoned his army to secure his political position, leaving his brother-in-law, the very stylish Marshal Joachim Murat, in charge. The tragi-comedy of errors was hardly done, though. Murat was the King of Naples, courtesy of Napoléon (obviously), and much like his benefactor, absence from the throne made his subjects fonder for just about anyone else. The King of Naples hightailed it back to the warmer climes of Italy and left Eugene de Beauharnais in charge. Eugene, just in case you're keeping score at home, was the son of Joséphine (divorced from Nappy in 1810) from her previous marriage to the guillotined General Alexandre de Beauharnais.

Out of the nearly seven hundred thousand men who started the campaign in June, only about forty thousand were present in ranks when Napoléon's former step-son led them across the Niemen River and out of Russian territory on December 12, 1812. Defeat. Disaster. Disloyalty. A typical French military outing. So commonplace, it's hardly worth noting.

It is not necessary for Napoleon to remain in Russia since we are all becoming "Boney!"

> "We have always been, we are, and I hope that we always shall be, detested in France."

—Arthur Wellesley, Duke of Wellington, victor at Waterloo

31
FROGS, FROGS, FROGS

Everyone refers to the French as Frogs. It hardly seems fair to insult a beneficial and attractive amphibian by comparing it to a band of pompous, foul-smelling cowards, but fairness is often in short supply when you eat flies for a living.

Calling Frenchmen frogs is hardly a recent thing, which makes finding the origin of the term difficult. Indeed, according to the Oxford English Dictionary, the term was originally used by the English as an insult for the Dutch. One suspects that the slur was deemed too useful for mere peons like the Dutch, and it was transferred over to a more suitable target: the French. So what follows are some possible rationalizations for the insult. Feel free to add your own.

1. The French fleur-de-lis, the emblem of French royalty, is said to resemble a frog.

2. The early Frankish kings used frogs and bees as symbols.

3. Another nickname for a Frenchman is Jean Crapaud: John Toad.

4. The French like to eat frogs.

5. The land around Paris was so swampy back in the day that the inhabitants were referred to as frogs.

6. Queen Elizabeth I had a French lover who she referred to as her "little frog."

7. Frenchmen croak like frogs.

8. Frenchmen look like frogs.

9. Frenchmen smell like frogs.

10. Frenchmen hop like frogs.

11. Frenchmen taste like frogs. [Editor: Enough already]

> "The French are the connecting link between man and the monkey."
>
> —Mark Twain

32

PROPOSED FRENCH NATIONAL ANTHEMS

"Born to Run" by Bruce Springsteen
"Hands Up" by Ottawan
"I Surrender" by Celine Dion
"Raise Your Hands" by Jon Bon Jovi
"Runaway" by Del Shannon
"Running Scared" by Roy Orbison
"Surrender" by Elvis Presley
"Sweet Surrender" by Sarah McLachlan
"Walk Right In" by the Rooftop Singers (only to be sung at events where Germans are present)

> *"And thirdly you must hate a Frenchman as you hate the devil."*
>
> —Admiral Horatio Nelson, victor over the French at Aboukir Bay and Trafalgar, being a bit unfair to Satan

33

CHOOSE YOUR ALLIES WISELY

Name: Ferdinand Maximilian Joseph, Archduke of Austria (1832-67)
Conflict: Mexican Adventure
Opponent: Mexican Republicans

Maximilian, Austrian archduke, French stooge
(*Maximiliano* by Pierre Guillaume Metzmacher)

DREARY DETAILS:

It must have seemed like a good idea at the time. There was Mexico, an economic basket case (Yes, that's redundant. We know.) devastated by the civil war of 1857-1861. There was Mexico, owing France, Great Britain and Spain a boatload of money. There was Mexico, just south of those idiot Americans, who were just too much like the hooligans from their mother country, perfidious Albion. *Et quelle chance!* The (idiot) Americans were distracted by their very own civil war and would have no chance to blather on about their silly Monroe Doctrine.

Yep. It must have seemed like a good idea at the time. For Napoléon III, founder of the Second Empire, what better way to strut his Bonapartist stuff than by adding a crappy hellhole to the imperial domain and increasing the glory of France (and the supply of reliable, hard-working lawn specialists who would happily toil away for the mere pittance of a slug of tequila)?

When Mexican President Benito Juarez suspended foreign debt payments (which totally wasn't his fault because those bitches in Guatemala decided to get their grass cut twice a month instead of every week and that really screwed up the budget, man), the European powers put their heads together and decided: "Let's occupy Mexico until we get our money back!" "Okay," replied Juarez, but the Europeans had to stay out of Mexican internal affairs. There is no record of whether any of the negotiators laughed aloud at that point.

By December 1861, a ten thousand–strong expeditionary force occupied Vera Cruz, but by April 1862, the Spaniards and British had had enough. The Brits probably realized why the Americans only kept the part north of the Rio Grande after the conquests of the Mexican-American War in 1846-48. The Spaniards undoubtedly remembered why they had never bothered to reconquer their former colony. It's the same reason they're all making a break for the border these days: Mexico sucks.

But Napoléon III was made of ~~sterner~~ stupider stuff. If his famous uncle could abandon armies and squander blood and treasure in Egypt, Spain, and Russia, then surely he could do the same in Burritostan. Call it OPL (Other People's Lives). By May 1862, the gloves were off. The French didn't want the debt payments; they decided to foreclose on the entire property. Even better, the (idiot) American Civil War now had all the makings of an epic barn-burner, the sort that would curse future generations with self-congratulatory memoirs, peevish novels, and god-awful television mini-series (Yeah, we're talking about you, Patrick Swayze).

Unfortunately, for the French, the tenants (to continue with the housing motif) had the bad grace to fight their eviction. It was not until May 1863 with the help of the Foreign Legion (see Chapter 48) that Mexico City fell.

Now that Mexico was under control (sorta, kinda), Napoléon III needed a fellow monarch to run the show. After all, no self-respecting republic would allow itself to be a pawn in the French Drive for World Domination ™. It had to be a monarchy, but not just any monarch would do. No pesky Bourbons or uppity Hohenzollerns need apply.

As luck would have it, the Hapsburgs of Austria just happened to have a spare archduke lying around. Enter Maximilian, who had been dismissed in 1859 by his brother, the Emperor Franz Josef I, from his post as the viceroy in Lombardy in Italy for ideals entirely too liberal for a royal. Of course, Franz Josef was so stodgy that, fifty years later, he would veto the introduction of tanks into the Austrian Army with the outburst, "The horses will be startled!", so heaven knows what would have constituted too liberal in his crabby mind. Coincidentally, in 1859, Mexican monarchists had approached Maximilian about a job opening, but things hadn't worked out back then as Max was too busy playing explorer in the forests of Brazil.

By 1863, having gotten the Junior Scientist bug out of his system, Maximilian was ready to assume the lofty position of French puppet. Not that Max was a dullard. By no means. He had been instrumental in the resurrection of the Austrian Navy in the 1850s and was trained as a botanist. However, he made the mistake never made by despots, potentates, and dictators in the know: Never trust the French. Regardless, he took the fatal plunge and was proclaimed Emperor of Mexico on April 10, 1864.

Deceived as to the level of popular support he could expect, Maximilian boarded a ship and set off for Mexico, never to return. He never had a honeymoon period. Mexican republicans refused to recognize his authority, and Maximilian quickly angered his monarchist allies by displaying the same liberal streak that had ticked off Franz Josef back in the home country. His refusal to revoke Juarez's land reforms won him no friends on the republican side and cost him dear support on the monarchist side. Even worse, by May 1865, the (idiot) American Civil War was essentially over, and the (idiot) Americans started gibbering on about the Monroe Doctrine and supplied the republican forces with weapons. It was enough for Napoléon III, faced with great political pressure back home, to give up the Great Mexican Adventure of a Lifetime. Not that it takes all that much to send a Frenchman scurrying for his mortal existence. By early 1867, the last French troops had vamoosed.

As for the Emperor Maximilian, he refused to take the hint. Noble to a fault, he refused to abandon those who had foolishly thrown in their lot with him. His army retreated from Mexico City to Queretaro on February 13, 1867, where it was besieged until the town fell on May 15.

Maximilian was captured, tried before a military tribunal, and sentenced to death. On June 19, Maximilian woke up for the final time and took the long walk to stand in front of a firing squad. No doubt he was cursing the French inside, but he made a manly show of it anyway.

Austrian Monarch + French Troops = Express Lane to Mexican Firing Squad

("Execution of Maximilian, Mejia, and Miramon at Quetaro, Mexico" from *Harper's Weekly*, August 16, 1867)

❝
"I like France, where everybody thinks he's Napoleon."
❞

—F. Scott Fitzgerald, *Tender is the Night*

34

A FLAG OF (IN)CONVENIENCE

Every army must have a battle flag.

Behold the French Tricolore in use since 1794. Very nice. Very colorful. (Yeah, yeah, so it's in black and white, but do you know how much it costs to print in color?)

Now, an army on the march is very sensitive to weight. Only the most essential gear is carried. Anything else (such as bowling balls, surf boards, rifles) will be discarded by the French soldier as useless. Even saving a few

A FLAG OF (IN)CONVENIENCE | 127

ounces can spell the difference between spending the war in a POW camp and failure.

Now, let's take another look at that Tricolore and see how our friends, the French, have cleverly retained a critical tool and saved precious grams in the process.

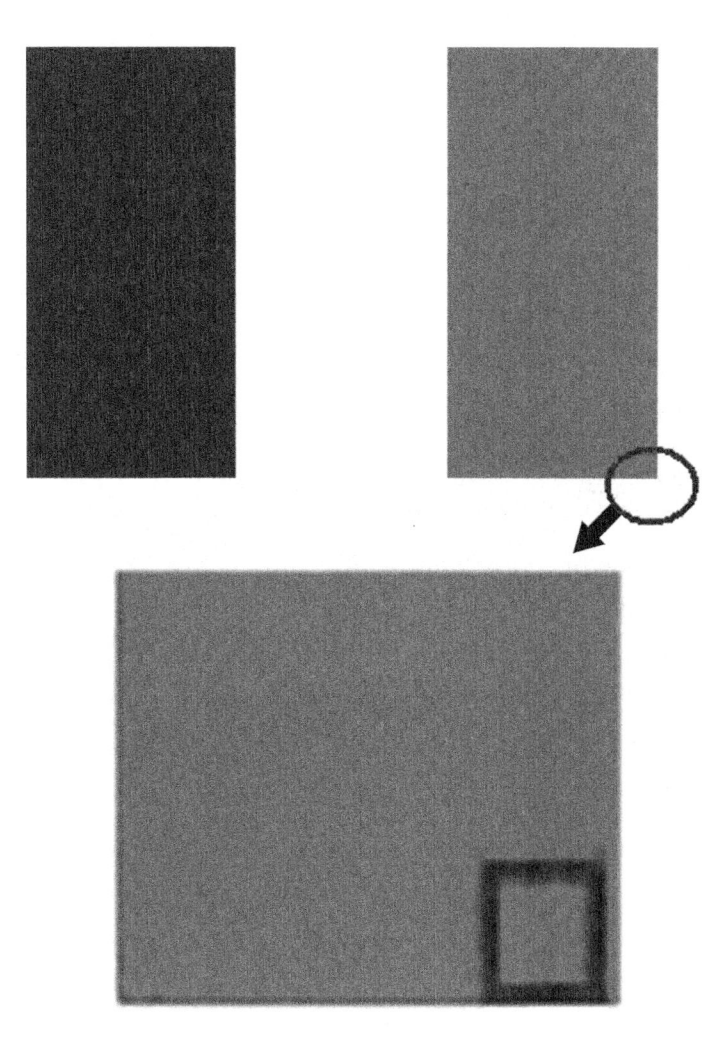

Velcro Tab

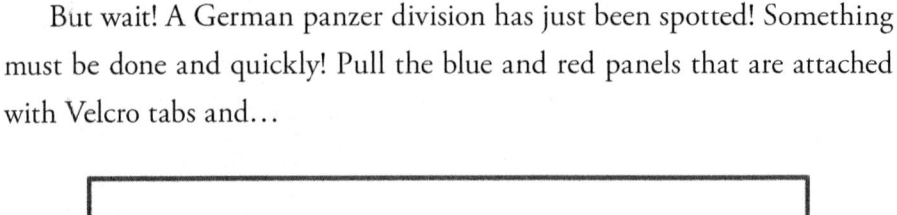

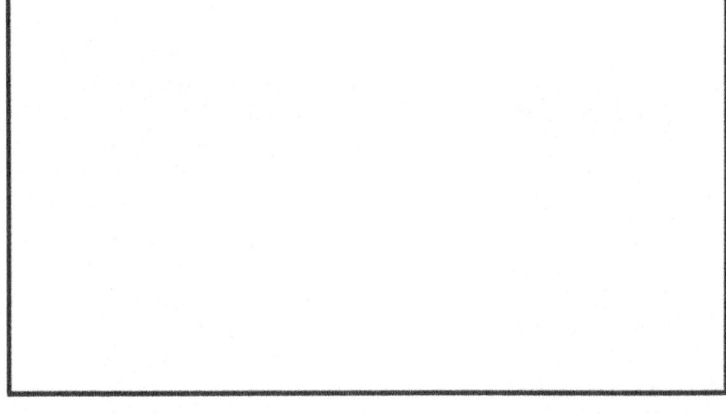

But wait! A German panzer division has just been spotted! Something must be done and quickly! Pull the blue and red panels that are attached with Velcro tabs and…

Voila! A fairly useless battle flag is transformed into a very useful surrender flag.

Thanks to this Gallic ingenuity, thousands of (non)fighting Frenchmen are now out of danger, sipping champagne in a prisoner of war camp outside of Dusseldorf.

Note that experienced soldiers will customize the white flag to reflect the campaign that they are on currently. Have a look:

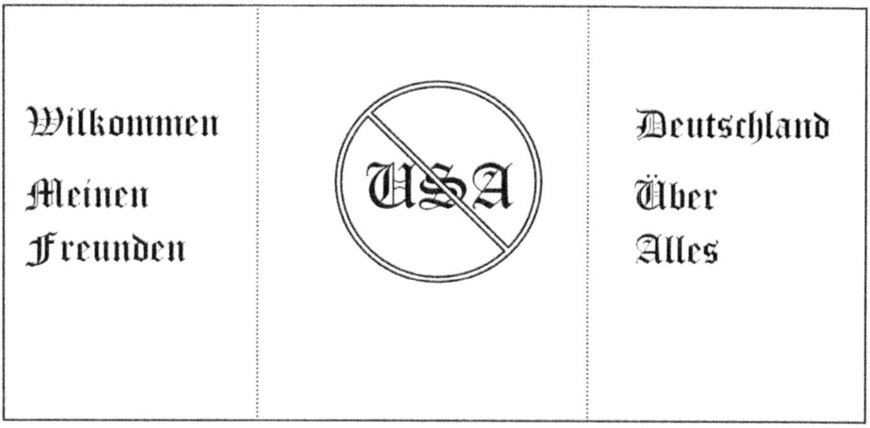
Wilkommen
Meinen
Freunden
USA
Deutschland
Über
Alles

"The last time the French asked for more proof, it came marching into Paris under a German flag."

— David Letterman, *Late Night*

35

THE UNCLE'S MONKEY

Fight: Franco-Prussian War
Date: July 19, 1870 – May 10, 1871
Opponents: Second Empire (Napoléon III, Emperor of France)
versus
Prussia (Wilhelm I, King of Prussia, and Otto von Bismarck, Chancellor of Prussia)
Incompetent French Leaders: Napoléon III, who mistook himself for his famous uncle, by taking command of the Army of the Rhine, and all his generals, who mistook themselves for that famous uncle's marshals
Outcome: Crushing French Defeat! Second Empire ends. Third Republic begins. Napoléon III exiled to England. What a disaster!

THE PATHETIC DETAILS:

With the execution of Maximilian in Mexico (see Chapter 33) and the Austrian defeat at the hands of the Prussians in 1866, Napoléon III began to fear for his nation's position in Europe as Otto von Bismarck and Wilhelm I stirred the pot in the quest for a greater unified Germany.

While Nappy Part 3 did not have his uncle's military talent, he certainly had his ambition, and his fondest desire was to expand France to include Belgium, Luxembourg, and the southern Netherlands, basically all of Europe west of the Rhine. Worst of all, *le nouveau* Napoléon had tossed out the Second Republic, but had forgotten to toss out the men who still wanted a republic. A war with Prussia would kill several birds with one stone: punish the Prussians, expand French territory, unite the French people behind the Bonapartist regime, and make France the wonder of Europe. (They're a wonder, all right.)

Both sides were spoiling for a fight, and soon found the *causus belli* (that's Latin for...something) when the Spanish throne came vacant again. The Spaniards offered the monarchy to a German prince, a certain Leopold, who just happened to be a distant cousin of Wilhelm. The French could not tolerate having Hohenzollern regimes on two borders and protested. Much to their surprise and disappointment, Wilhelm agreed and had Leopold's name withdrawn.

But wars always have their way. On July 13, 1870, Count Vincent Benedetti, the ambassador to Prussia, delivered the French demand that Wilhelm I never allow another Hohenzollern candidate to be presented for the Spanish throne. The Kaiser's incensed telegram about this impertinent interview was edited and then leaked by Bismarck to the international press with the intention of insulting the French. He succeeded, and the French declared war on July 19.

NOTABLE DISASTER:

So many to choose from. Of course, there's the Battle of Sedan that saw most of the French Army destroyed and Napoléon III captured. That's pretty bad. The head of state and one hundred thousand men captured. So if that's not the disaster being chosen, you know something has got to be much worse.

For sheer demonstration of French incompetence, it's hard to beat the Battle of Mars-La-Tour on August 16, 1870. The Prussian III Corps, outnumbered four to one, that's right four to one, prevented the 130,000 man Army of the Rhine from retreating to Verdun. This gallant effort by the beleaguered Prussians forced the French forces back into their fortresses at Metz, where they were immediately besieged. This siege ultimately led to Napoléon's relief effort and defeat at Sedan.

French wanna-be chats with Prussian real-deal

(*Napoleon III and Bismarck on the Morning after the Battle of Sedan, 1870* by Wilhelm Camphausen)

> "Shoot and stab all the French, down to the little babies."
>
> — Johanna von Bismarck, wife of the famous Prussian prime minister, expressing a most admirable sentiment (one suspects that the Bismarck breakfast table had some interesting conversations)

36

HOW DO YOU SAY "SCAPEGOAT" IN FRENCH?

> *Name:* Captain Alfred Dreyfus
> *Conflict:* L'Affaire Dreyfus
> *Opponents:* Dreyfusards versus Anti-Dreyfusards

DREARY DETAILS:

Like many other societies in the world, France was and is one of those places that, when things are going poorly, the someone who gets blamed tends to be Jewish.

And like most things that bedevil the French, it all started with the Germans. After the industrial-strength beat-down they received in the Franco-Prussian War (see Chapter 35), the French intelligence (how's that for an oxymoron?) services spent a great deal of effort tracking the goings on at the German embassy in Paris. Given the Gallic propensity for laziness, it probably meant tracking the fiendish Hun for twenty-five hours a week instead of the usual fifteen.

One of the great coups of the secret service was recruiting a cleaning woman inside the embassy who would bring the boys scraps of paper found in trash bins and any leftover bottles of schnapps. One day, in September 1894, Madame Housekeeper brought them an anonymous letter (referred to forever after as the *bordereau*) that promised the Germans the delivery of documents relating to French troop dispositions, Madagascar, which the French were intent on invading to compensate for their strategic deficiency in lemurs, and the recoil mechanism of a new artillery piece.

Alarmed at this revelation, several army officers began the hunt for the traitor. This group, led by Lieutenant Colonel Faber, concluded that the culprit must have been a staff officer and went through the rolls until they came to a name that Faber remembered: Captain Alfred Dreyfus. Faber recalled that the Jewish officer had served in his office the prior year and had received bad marks from him. It was enough.

The investigators procured a sample of Dreyfus's handwriting and had a forgery expert for the Bank of France compare it with the *bordereau*. The expert pronounced that Dreyfus probably was not their man, which led them to another "expert" in the police department who gave the desired opinion. The Minister of War Auguste Mercier gave the order to arrest the most unfortunate Captain Dreyfus.

In an episode that could only occur in French real-life or television or film or theatre, Dreyfus was summoned to the War Ministry on October 15 in civilian clothes. There, he was met by a certain Major Du Paty de Clam (you just can't make this stuff up), who, feigning a hand injury, asked Dreyfus to take dictation for him. Du Paty recited the very documents promised in the anonymous *bordereau*. The Major was so convinced that his clever plan would work its magic that he left a loaded pistol on the table next to the accused, so the Jewish miscreant could settle the matter in an honorable manner; apparently, it never occurred to the good major that a desperate spy (and an untrustworthy Jew, at that) might take the gun and shoot his way to freedom, but, then again, this is why an entire massively best-selling book on French military disasters can be written and transport its author from part-time toll booth attendant to wealth beyond imagination.

Surprisingly, shockingly, Du Paty's cheap theatrics did not have the desired effect, and Dreyfus had to be hauled off to prison the old-fashioned way, where his confinement was kept secret until actual proof of his guilt could be manufactured…err…found. Unfortunately for Mercier, no such proof was forthcoming. Dreyfus apparently wasn't the chummiest fellow, but he led an exemplary life, and his family had money (of course, he had money; he was a Jew!), which wrecked any financial motives for the alleged treason.

Even worse, the secret arrest became public knowledge in late October, and the unwashed French masses howled for Dreyfus's head on a platter. The obscure captain of artillery was cast as the bogeyman responsible for whatever vile and treacherous acts that had not already been assigned to the English, Germans, Americans, or UFOs. Mercier now realized that the drama could only have two possible outcomes: Dreyfus goes to jail, or Mercier loses his job. Well, this is all very predictable, *non*? *C'est dommage, Monsieur Dreyfus.*

Dreyfus's trial lasted four days. He was convicted on December 22, 1894 and sentenced to life imprisonment on Devil's Island in French Guyana. Several months later, as he was ritualistically removed from the army, General Darras proclaimed, "You are degrading an innocent man!"

Nevertheless, Dreyfus's sword was broken in half, and all his decorations and insignia were ripped from his uniform. Mercier's victory was short-lived: When the French Cabinet was reshuffled in January 1895, he was not asked to return. The Dreyfus Affair had just claimed its second victim.

The first victim (Dreyfus himself) was bundled off to the sweltering, disease-ridden hell of ~~Detroit~~ Devil's Island, arriving there on March 15, 1895. However, he was not forgotten, and troubling questions lingered in the wake of his departure. The first to take action was the new head of the Intelligence Office, Lieutenant Colonel Georges Picquart, who not only concluded that Dreyfus was innocent, but also identified the correct culprit: Major Ferdinand Walsin Esterhazy, a ne'er-do-well with a taste for gambling. He raised his concerns and met a level of stonewalling and conspiracy that would seem improbable, even on an episode of *The X-Files*. As Picquart pressed for action, he made himself a marked man. He recalled the following conversation with Deputy Chief of Staff General Charles-Arthur Gonse:

> Gonse: What can it matter to you whether this Jew remains at Devil's Island or not?
>
> Picquart: But he is innocent.
>
> Gonse: That is an affair that cannot be reopened. General Mercier and General Saussier are involved in it.
>
> Piquart: Still, what would be our position if the family ever found out the real culprit?
>
> Gonse: If you say nothing, nobody will ever know it.
>
> Piquart: What you have just said is abominable, General. I do not know yet what course I shall take, but in any case, I will not carry this secret with me to the grave.

Shortly, thereafter, Picquart was assigned to a posting in Tunis to get him out of the way. He was now victim number three.

However, the reassignment did not work. Realizing the danger that he was in, Picquart decided to let more folks in on the secret, which he did while on a leave to Paris. He was able to gain the ear of a sympathetic politician, Auguste Scheurer-Kestner, vice-president of the Senate.

What followed was a wild flurry of forged documents and telegrams, one of which almost sent Picquart back into the North African wilderness, but ultimately ended in Dreyfus's brother Matthew publicly denouncing Major Esterhazy in November 1897.

The seemingly obscure court-martial of an obscure artillery captain laid bare deep divisions in the French body politic on matters like republicanism versus monarchism, clericalism versus secularism, and the nation split between *dreyfusards* and *antidreyfusards*. Esterhazy's acquittal in a sham court-martial did little to relieve the tension.

Enter stage left, famed novelist Emile Zola. On January 13, 1898, his legendary essay *J'accuse* (I accuse) appeared in the newspaper *L'Aurore* (French for The Bore). Zola pulled out the verbal big stick and took on the entire corrupt enterprise surrounding the Dreyfus Affair. Like most Frenchmen, he couldn't immediately come to the point, but among the zingers in the essay:

> "I accuse General Mercier of complicity, at least by mental weakness, in one of the great inequities of the century." Biff!

> "I accuse General Billot of having held in his hands absolute proof of Dreyfus's innocence..." Zowie!

"I accuse the War Office of using the press.... to conduct an abominable campaign to mislead the public and cover up their own wrongdoing." Zoink!

He then concluded by acknowledging that he may have been in violation of the libel laws.

On this point, he was not mistaken, and Zola's trial for libel turned into a circus. Zola's opponents distinguished themselves with pithy comments like "Kill the Jews!" Zola was found guilty and like a typical Frog ran like a big sissy to England, but the proceedings had allowed Picquart to finally testify in public and brought many questions about Dreyfus to the surface.

At long last, things moved the unfortunate captain's way. Esterhazy was arrested for forgery and drummed out of the army. Esterhazy's accomplice, Major Henry, had committed suicide. Politicians opposed to revisiting the case left office. Dreyfus was recalled from Devil's Island in June 1899 and appeared before a new court-martial in August, where he was once again found guilty, but with "extenuating circumstances," a waffle that would make even a Belgian proud. It was enough, though, and ~~the treacherous Jew~~ Dreyfus was pardoned. He walked out of prison on September 20, 1899, free at last. Ultimate exoneration would not come until 1906 when he was allowed back into the army. However, the hard feelings did not go away. When Zola's ashes were moved to the Pantheon in 1908, Dreyfus was shot and slightly wounded in the arm by a journalist (and we think the lame-stream media in the United States is biased).

The last laugh belonged to Picquart, who ultimately became the Minister of War.

It would not be the last time that France would have to deal with the specter of nationalism merged with anti-Semitism (see Vichy France in Chapter 42).

> *"France did the dirty work pretty much on its own, often anticipating and even out-doing the Nazis at the job of anti-Semitism."*
>
> —Professor Richard Weisberg, testimony before the U.S. House of Representatives, Committee on Banking and Financial Services, September 1999

"A Family Dinner" from *Le Figaro*, February 14, 1898
Top panel: "Above all, let us not discuss the Dreyfus Affair."
Bottom panel: "They have discussed it."

37

FUN FACTS ABOUT FÉLIX FRANÇOIS FAURE

It was February 16, 1899, and President Félix François Faure was up to his eyeballs with the Dreyfus Affair (see Chapter 36). The antechamber to his office at the Élysée Palace was unusually crowded as Monsieur Le Président (Triple F to *son amis*) kept his appointments waiting. Suddenly, the door to Faure's office flung open. The urgent cry for a doctor rang out.

Félix François Faure was dead.

Turns out that while the functionaries of state and business were cooling their heels out in the waiting room, the fifty-seven-year old Faure was tending to more pressing matters with the alluring Madame Marguerite Steinheil, twenty-seven years his junior, wife of a well-known artist. All France mourned the passing of the great man, the seventh president of the Third Republic, complete with japes about *la pompe funébre* (and you don't have to know any French to get the gist of *pompe*) and all sorts of other sexual puns.

And what does this have to do with the epic defeats of the French military? Not a damn thing except to remind us of how exceptionally amoral, deviant, oversexed, and, frankly, unhealthy the Frogs are. Really. You should discuss your general health status with your doctor to ensure that you are healthy enough to engage in sexual activity.

> "A dead Frenchman has many good qualities, many things to recommend him; many attractions—even innocences. Why cannot we have more of these?"

—Mark Twain

38

HELL, NO! WE WON'T GO!

Conflict: World War I (aka The Great War aka The War to End All Wars aka All These Deaths Just to Save France? Really?)
Dates: 1914 - 1918
Incompetent French Leader: General Robert Nivelle
Notable Disaster: The Great Mutiny

PATHETIC DETAILS:

Every military has had to face down the specter of mutiny at some point during its history. Unpopular wars, brutal leaders, long separations from home, awful food. It all adds up, and, on top of that having someone trying to kill you! Even Alexander the Great's men rose up against him in India. Of course, they had conquered most of their known world, so they could be forgiven for wanting to go back home to the couch and take a load off.

However, when it comes to mass dereliction of duty, it is difficult to top the events that plagued the French Army in the spring of 1917.

As most know, unless you received your history education in an American public school, the Western Front during World War I had been locked in the deadly stalemate of trench warfare ever since the British and French checked the German offensive at the First Battle of the Marne in September 1914. From then on, both sides alternated bludgeoning each other in a series of ill-conceived attacks that began with thunderous, days-long artillery bombardments, followed by mass infantry charges across fields pulverized into a muddy slurry, which invariably failed in a hailstorm of machine gunfire. The generals, puzzled at their lack of success, vowed to use more artillery and infantry next time.

The "next time" in question occurred in April 1917, when the French commander-in-chief, General Robert Nivelle launched a spring offensive that promptly floundered in the mire of the Aisne River valley. The first week of the campaign saw one hundred thousand casualties, but Nivelle continued the attack, insisting that a breakthrough was at hand. Little did he anticipate the break that was about to happen.

The first inkling of trouble occurred on the night of April 29 when an infantry battalion refused to return to the front. Drunk and angry, the soldiers would not budge, but, after they sobered up, military discipline prevailed. Officers reacted swiftly to punish the mutineers, but it was too late. On May 3, the entire Second Division decided that their participation in the war was now optional. And from there, the mutiny bug spread from unit to unit, cheap wine being the lubricant, until virtually the entire French Army on the front lines was rendered combat ineffective. Nivelle's Offensive was over, Nivelle himself was over, and the Germans were still on French soil, a mere sixty miles from Paris.

General Henri Pétain took over from Nivelle on May 15 and halted all offensive activities. Despite the change in leadership, the mutinies continued into June, where sixteen different divisions were affected. The men complained of poor food, lack of leave, and the senseless slaughter. Officers were assaulted, camps were ransacked, and soldiers fought each other in alcohol-fueled melees. Pétain concluded that the French Army was not able to fight at all as the mutiny had affected sixty-eight out of 112 divisions. Some reports suggest that Pétain thought he could only rely on two of his divisions to resist the Germans.

Pétain instituted several reforms, most notably allowing more generous home leave. He also cracked down on the leaders of the mutiny, and, if no leader could be found in a particular unit, every tenth soldier was chosen and punished. By September, the mutiny had run its course. Over three thousand men had been found guilty at court-martial and received sentences ranging from execution to short imprisonment. Around fifty mutineers paid the ultimate price.

Undoubtedly, the conditions of the French Army in the trenches were deplorable, and the unthinking actions of officers like Nivelle did little to convince the hard-pressed *poilu* that he was anything but a sheep being led to slaughter. Nevertheless, the Mutiny of 1917 is one of the lowlights in the history of an army with a lot of bad moments. The French Army quit on its own turf and left the heavy-lifting to the British and Canadians up in Flanders, who launched the bloody Battle of Passchendaele in July 1917 to draw German attention away from the prostrate French divisions.

As for the Germans, they received intelligence telling them that the French forces were racked by dissension, but they failed to take advantage of the situation. Why? They couldn't believe that an entire European army could possibly be suffering from such a breakdown in discipline. If only this book had been around back then to guide them.

How did I know the secret plan for the offensive, mon General?
It's the same as all of our previous attacks.

> "I don't know why people are surprised that France won't help us get Saddam out of Iraq. After all, France wouldn't help us get the Germans out of France!"

— Jay Leno, *The Tonight Show*

39
THINGS NEVER HEARD AT ALLIED HQ

We could never picture Eisenhower saying any of the following:

1. I've assigned the French to secure [fill in blank]

    a. Our flanks

    b. Our supply routes

    c. Our latrines

2. It's the French! The day is saved!

3. Go tell it to the French.

4. The French position is so secure the Germans would never attack there.

5. Boy, there's nothing like a good Chardonnay.

6. Get De Gaulle in here! I need his advice on [fill in blank]

    a. Whipping up a soufflé to impress Montgomery

    b. Scoring with the French babes once we liberate Paris

    c. Preparing the unconditional surrender documents for those Nazi bastards! (Okay, that one might have happened.)

7. American leadership, French troops. An unbeatable combination.

8. French leadership, American troops. An unbeatable combination.

9. What do you mean we can't shoot the French? (Okay, this too might have been uttered.)

10. Hey, these frog legs taste like chicken.

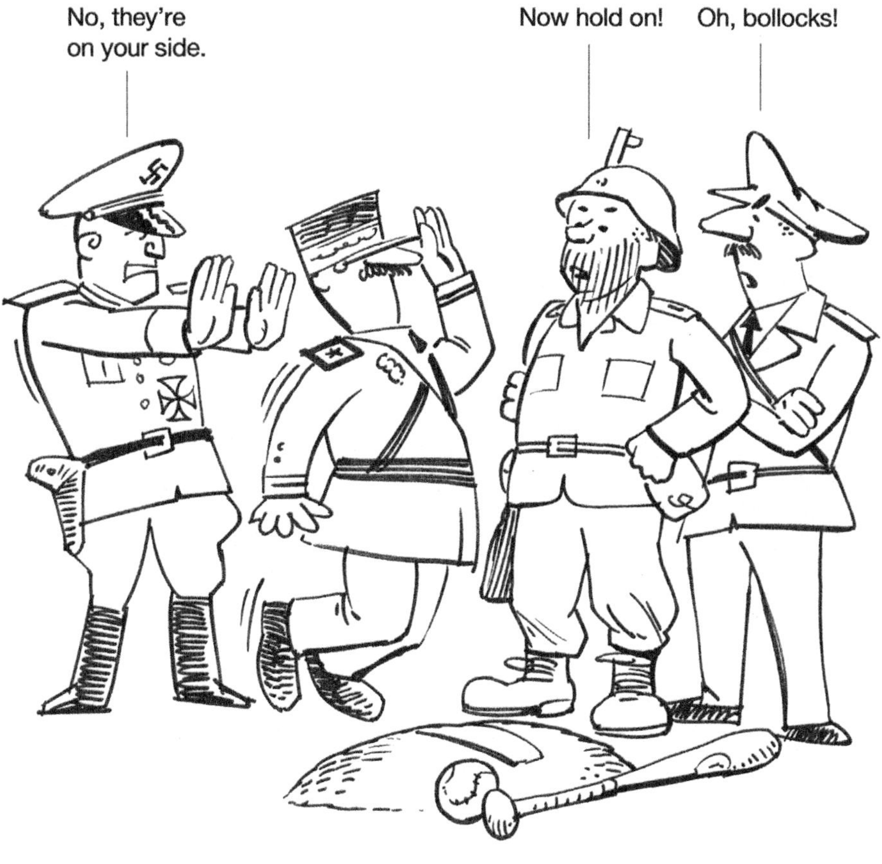
No, they're on your side.
Now hold on!
Oh, bollocks!

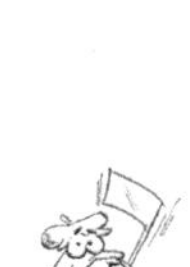

> "Of all the crosses I have had to bear during this war, the heaviest has been the Cross of Lorraine [symbol of the Free French]."
>
> —Major General Edward Spears, Churchill's envoy to the Free French, about his difficulties in working with General Charles de Gaulle

40

LE DEUXIÈME GUERRE MONDIALE

Fight:	World War II
Date:	September 3, 1939–June 22, 1940
Opponents:	Third Republic
	versus
	Nazi Germany
Incompetent French Leaders:	Maurice Gamelin, Supreme Commander, French Forces
	Paul Reynaud, French Prime Minister
Outcome:	Holy moly, if you thought the Franco-Prussian debacle was bad, there are no words to describe this. Third Republic destroyed. Allies barely notice the loss.

PATHETIC DETAILS:

When Germany invaded Poland on September 1, 1939, the British and French, finally realizing that the occupations of Austria, Czechoslovakia, and now Poland constituted a trend of sorts, promptly declared war. What ensued was the sort of combat that the Frogs have traditionally excelled in: no fighting whatsoever. The French Army marched into German territory, but, by September 12, after an exhausting five miles in, the Frogs did an about-face and headed home. No German forces, not a single soldier, airplane, panzer, or dachshund, were diverted from neutralizing the Polish menace, and Warsaw fell on September 28.

Then, a quiet descended on Western Europe. Observers foolishly called it the Phony War, though with World War I as the most recent example of carnage, we can cut them some slack for not recognizing that the light they saw at the end of the tunnel was actually an onrushing locomotive.

On May 10, 1940, the Germans roared out of the Ardennes Forest and demonstrated that the only thing "phony" about this war was the French Army, which collapsed like a soufflé in the rain. General Gamelin could not believe that the Germans were not gamely repeating their efforts from World War I and immediately set to work on a strongly worded letter of protest. However, he was observant enough to note that the French were suffering from "inferiority of numbers, inferiority of equipment, inferiority of method." Prime Minister Reynaud, in one of the all-time great heroic conversations, told Winston Churchill, "We have been defeated. We are beaten. We have lost the battle." This inspirational phone call took place on May 15. The Germans had entered French territory on…May 13.

In any case, if Churchill had any doubts as to how the battle was going in the French mind, he could not help but notice, during his May 16 visit to Paris that evacuation plans were being made and archives were being put to the torch. Seeing that the French were no longer in the game, the British Expeditionary Force evacuated the Continent from Dunkirk on May 26. Paris gave up without a fight on June 10. The French surrendered on June 22. What Wilhelm II could not accomplish in four gruesome years, Hitler managed in six fun-filled weeks against a foe with numerical and qualitative advantages in manpower, armor, aircraft, and ships.

Absolutely pathetic, even by French standards.

There is almost certainly at least one Frenchman who will write a letter of protest if we invade.

> "Looking back, I may be permitted once more to state that it was not Germany in September, 1939, which declared war on France or Britain, but that on the contrary I have scarcely permitted an occasion to pass since taking over power to convert relations precisely between Germany and France from the strain of the Versailles dictate into truly friendly collaboration."

—Adolf Hitler, in a letter to Marshal Philippe Pétain, November 27, 1942 (say what you will about Dolf, but he sure had the Frogs pegged)

41

THE CURIOUS CASE OF THE FRENCH BATTLESHIPS

Fight:	World War II
Dates:	July 3, 1940 and November 8, 1942
Opponents:	Vichy France versus
	United Kingdom
	United States
Incompetent French Leaders:	Admiral Marcel-Bruno Gensoul (Mers-el-Kebir)
	Captain Emile Barthes (Casablanca)
Outcome:	French humiliated yet again. British and American Navies win, but it's kind of like when Alabama plays Sweet Briar in football. Just not a lot of glory there.

PATHETIC DETAILS:

An understandably overlooked aspect of the 1940 debacle, given the incandescent triumph of German armored tactics, was the fate of the French Navy.

Fearful (that word sure comes up a lot when you write about the French) of their homeports being overrun, the Frog Navy hopped over to the colonies in North Africa. However, knowing the French as well as he did, Churchill understood that was hardly the end of the matter and that it was now the Royal Navy's turn to worry. Hard-pressed with the U-boat campaign in the North Atlantic, the Italian fleet in the Mediterranean, air attacks on Malta, and rumblings from the Japanese in the Pacific, the last thing the Brits needed was for the French fleet to wind up in the pay of Adolph Hitler.

The British demanded the French ships either join them or intern themselves somewhere the Germans couldn't get their grubby paws on them. The French, suddenly discovering their martial spirit, refused. As long as untrustworthy Frogs splashed around the Mediterranean unsupervised, a fight was inevitable.

NOTABLE DISASTERS:

Embarrassment #1 - Operation Catapult

On July 3, 1940, the British decided to do something about the French problem. French ships in British ports like Portsmouth and Alexandria were boarded. However, the largest group of Vichy ships under Admiral Gensoul was in its home port at Mers-el-Kebir in Algeria. This fleet consisted of two old battleships, two modern battlecruisers and thirteen destroyers.

The British, being the British and having a habit of crushing French naval forces just for sport, did what they usually did in such cases: they kicked in the front door. Force H under Admiral James Somerville sailed straight into the harbor and attacked. Unusually, the British made a hash of the operation, only sinking the ancient battleship *Bretagne*. They managed to damage *Dunkerque* and *Provence*, but those ships and the remainder of the French fleet somehow managed to escape back to Toulon.

Churchill had let Germany and the United States know that Great Britain had no intention of quitting the fight. Obviously, the Frogs would have preferred that British tenacity be demonstrated somewhere else, preferably on German targets. Incensed, the Vichy government spoke of throwing in their lot with the Nazis, more so than what they were already doing by hunting down Jews, but more sensible heads prevailed. Still, they got the message, and, when the Germans finally made their move to grab the remaining French ships in Toulon on November 27, 1942, they were all scuttled.

French destroyer *Mogador* burns after running aground at Mers-el-Kebir

Embarrassment #2- Operation Torch

Even more bizarre were the events that transpired in Casablanca on November 8, 1942. American forces were scheduled to land in Morocco as part of Operation *Torch* with the intention of driving east to link up with Field Marshal Bernard Montgomery's plodding British Eighth Army to smash Erwin Rommel's Afrika Korps between them.

The only hang-up was that the French weren't having any part of it. Perhaps compensating for their no-show on the home field back in Frogistan, the Worst Navy in the World™ prepared to defend North Africa for dishonesty, oppression, and the Parisian way. Confronting the U.S. landing was a small naval force centered on the brand-new *Richelieu*-class battleship *Jean Bart*, which had heretofore escaped the loving attention of the Royal Navy. Actually, this was probably because the ship was a little too brand new. So much so that her rangefinders, radar, and one of the main turrets did not function. To make it even less interesting, the French dreadnought was completely immobile, tied to the pier. Nevertheless, the plucky (read stupid) warship gamely decided to give battle.

What ensued would be one of the more (ahem) unusual battles in the annals of naval warfare as USS *Massachusetts* (BB-59) pounded the bejeezus out of the hapless French battleship. The American dreadnought also sank two destroyers and destroyed an ammunition dump for good measure. With things seemingly in hand, *Massachusetts* reported the coast was clear.

Not satisfied with that beating, *Jean Bart* would fire on and miss USS *Augusta* (CA- 31) two days later. That brought in an air attack from USS *Ranger* (CV-4). The ensuing damage left *Jean Bart* settled on the harbor bottom, but still upright.

The *Torch* landings proceeded with little incident.

Lest the reader is left thinking the two incidents described here encompass the whole of Allied distrust of the Vichy Navy, it is useful to remember that the United States and the United Kingdom sank thirty-one French naval vessels during the course of the war including one battleship, one light cruiser, ten destroyers, and fourteen submarines. By the way, that's seventeen more French ships than the Germans, Italians, and Japanese (you know, the chaps on the other side, the enemy, the Axis, the bad guys) had to send to the bottom.

On June 30, 1944, the submarine USS *Flasher* (SS-249) sank the French gunboat *Tahure* off the coast of Vietnam. Four years after the fall of France, the Allies were through hunting down the Vichy Navy.

> "While the great inarticulate and leaderless mass of the French people remain hopeful of a British victory and continue to hope that America will rescue them from their present predicament without their doing anything for themselves, the Government of France today, headed by a feeble, frightened old man [Marshal Philippe Pétain] surrounded by a group which probably for its own safety, is devoted to the Axis philosophy."

—Admiral William Leahy, American ambassador to Vichy France, in a letter to President Roosevelt, November 22, 1941

42

OH, THOSE VICHY

On June 22, 1940, the French surrendered to the Germans. In a mere six weeks, German armored doctrine had made a mockery of France's slavish devotion to defensive tactics and fixed fortifications. A mere six weeks for the largest army in Europe to demonstrate its intellectual and moral bankruptcy. A mere six weeks to be absolutely thrashed when they held the advantages in manpower, artillery, armor, naval force, and the intangible asset of fighting on home turf.

At Compiègne, Hitler had the last laugh as he had the armistice signed in the very railcar used to end World War I on November 11, 1918. It seemed that France had sunk as low as it possibly could. So it seemed.

But what happened afterwards was a disgusting mixture of anti-Semitic thuggery and collaboration, a fascist disgrace that France has ever after tried to bury in the history books, insisting that the Free French of Charles de Gaulle were the norm.

Here are some of the lowlights:

- Marshal Philippe Pétain, hero of World War I, served as head of the Vichy regime, lending it his military credentials and moral authority, minimal as those might be for the French. This would roughly be the equivalent of President Dwight D. Eisenhower throwing in with the Communists during the height of the Cold War.

- Pierre Laval, who served in various important roles in the Vichy government, was a three-time prime minister. Rather telling that a legitimate French politician found life so cozy with the Nazis.

- In October 1940, all French Jews were required to register with police.

- Vichy propaganda was vehemently anti-British, never anti-German.

- Vichy politicians came perilously close on several occasions to openly joining the German cause.

- Vichy French forces resisted Allied efforts in Morocco, Syria, and Madagascar.

- More Vichy Navy ships were sunk by the Allies than the Axis (thirty-one to fourteen).

- Joseph Darnand, head of the *Milice* (the Vichy Gestapo) and minister of the interior, also held rank in the infamous German *Schutzstaffel* (SS).

- Seventy-five thousand French Jews were deported to German concentration camps.

- In the infamous *Vélodrome d'hiver* (Winter Velodrome) raid of July 1942, not only did the French police round up all the Jews requested by the Germans, they tossed in 4,051 children that weren't requested just for the heck of it. Do you know how hard it is to find good henchmen, especially in wartime?

- The *Milice* was regarded as especially ruthless when dealing with their own countrymen involved in La Résistance.

We have a plan to help you round up the Jews.
No advice necessary!
Der Final Plan
L'Affaire Dreyfus

> *"France is entirely disposed to help Germany win the war [World War II if you're keeping score at home]."*
>
> —Admiral François Darlan, Vichy Minister of Defense, Foreign Affairs and Interior

43

MYTH BUSTER #3

MYTH: France is a staunch ally of the United States.
TRUTH: Forgive us if we laugh at you unmercifully and point you to a quote attributed to Charles de Gaulle, first president of the Fifth Republic:

> *"You may be sure that the Americans will commit all the stupidities they can think of, plus some that are beyond imagination."*

There you have it. Heartfelt gratitude for rescuing the miserable bastards from the Nazi menace.

Now, most of us seem to remember that the French helped us out in the American Revolution, but usually overlooked is the event that occurred barely a decade after our country was founded: the XYZ Affair.

The Frogs were going through their own revolution, beheading each other at a rapid rate to prove their devotion to notions such as liberty, fraternity, and egality. For some reason, perhaps afraid that the French were not slaughtering themselves quickly enough, the rest of Europe decided to join in the fun and declared war on France.

Now, this is where we come in. Thanks to Jay's Treaty (also known as the Treaty of Amity, Commerce, and Navigation, Between His Britannic Majesty and the United States of America) of 1794, we were back to trading with our hated cousins, the Brits, and the French thought this was very unsporting of us. After all, we were supposed to be French allies, and here we were doing business with their enemy, Perfidious Albion. Incensed, the Frogs started seizing our ships on the open seas, and there wasn't much we could do about it. Sadly, we didn't have much of a navy back then, so we decided to talk our way out of this situation.

President John Adams sent Charles Pinckney, John Marshall, and Elbridge Gerry to negotiate some sort of peaceful solution to the Frogs grabbing our ships. In March 1797, at a meeting in Paris, three French agents, whimsically referred to as X, Y, and Z, presented the following demands to our diplomatic dream team:

1. Fifty thousand pound bribe to the three agents

2. Ten million dollar loan to the state of France

3. Formal apology from President Adams

4. Two hundred, fifty thousand dollar bribe to French Foreign Minister Charles de Talleyrand

And all of that had to happen before the negotiations could even begin! Our boys told the insolent Frogs to shove it. Americans don't play games like that (at least, until we elected Barack Obama). Legend has it that Mr. Pinckney said, "Millions for defense, sir, but not one cent for tribute." However, recent research suggests that Pinckney actually said, "Bite my ass, Frenchie." We got busy building a navy, and the Quasi War would begin a year later. Franco-American relations have pretty much been downhill ever since.

Okay, one could argue that the XYZ Affair is ancient history, so let's see what the French have done for us since 1945:

- 1948-51—France receives over $2.2 billion in Marshall Plan expenditures, second most among recipients. (Our bust! That's what we did for them!)

- 1945-1962—Despite our warning them, the Frogs attempt to regain control of those uppity colonies that sort of went astray during all that German unpleasantness (otherwise known as World War II).

- 1950-53—During the Korean War, France contributes only one thousand soldiers out of nearly one million troops on the Allied side. (Guess we should be thankful they didn't send the thousand to the Communist side.) However, in all fairness, they were busy losing their fight in Vietnam.

- 1954—Frogs have the unmitigated gall to ask us to intervene in Vietnam during the disaster at Dien Bien Phu (see Chapter 47). Ike tells them to shove off.

- 1956—Frogs have a go at the Suez Canal (see Chapter 49). Ike tells them to shove off.

- 1958-69—De Gaulle attempts to chart a foreign policy that would establish France as a focal point for Third World countries not interested in aligning with either the United States or the Soviet Union. Oddly enough, there were no takers.

- March 1959—Frogistan removes its Mediterranean fleet from NATO command.

- June 1959—France announces it will not allow foreign nuclear weapons on its territory, forcing two hundred American aircraft to relocate.

- June 1963—France removes its Atlantic fleet from NATO command.

- 1966—France leaves NATO. All non-French troops depart from France. NATO headquarters moves from Paris to Brussels. This bold demonstration of independence occurs behind a wall of American, British, and German troops on the east bank of the Rhine that screens the west bank posturing of the Gaullists.

- April 1986—The French refuse overflight permission to American bombers targeting Libyan targets (Operation *El Dorado Canyon*) in retaliation for a nightclub bombing directed at American soldiers in Germany.

- 2002—The book *L'Effroyable Imposture* (The Horrifying Fraud) by Thierry Meyssan is published. The book alleges that the 9/11 attacks were perpetrated by the U.S. military. Though the author's ludicrous assertions are easily refuted by numerous authorities (and common sense), the book becomes a best-seller in France. However, given their own habit of blowing up things covertly (see Chapter 51), one can hardly fault the French for thinking we'd do the same.

- March 2003—French obstruct United States efforts against Iraq. George W. tells them to shove off.

Don't misunderstand us. France is not the 51st state. The French are not Americans (thank God). They are a sovereign nation that must pursue what they believe is best for their interests. But don't delude yourself into thinking that they are on our side. *Vive Mickey Mouse!*

> "What lessons would those be, M. Jospin? Scrap the Electoral College? Move to a system of direct presidential election? Tear up the Constitution and re-write it every generation, as the French do? Where are you up to now? Fifth Republic? Sixth Republic? Geez, get me an Al Gore lawyer: I need a manual recount of French constitutions."

—Mark Steyn, American political commentator, on French criticisms of the 2000 American presidential election

44
MAGINOT MUSINGS

M. André Maginot, French Minister of War in 1924. Too bad the line of fortifications named after him weren't as formidable as his moustaches.

> "We could hardly dream of building a kind of Great Wall of France, which would in any case be far too costly. Instead, we have foreseen powerful but flexible means of organizing defense, based on the dual principle of taking full advantage of the terrain and establishing a continuous line of fire everywhere."

—André Maginot, who at least had the good sense to die of typhoid fever in 1932 so he didn't have to live through the humiliation of seeing his name reduced to a synonym for failure on a colossal scale

> "If you entrench yourself behind strong fortifications, you compel the enemy to seek a solution elsewhere."

—Clausewitz, anticipating M. Maginot by a century

> "What can they [the Germans] do against the Maginot Line?"

—Léon Blum, three-time Prime Minister, who would spend most of World War II in the German concentration camp system after he learned the answer to his own question

"So that's what they can do against the Maginot Line!"

45
FOR SALE

Tourist? Collaborator? Learn German!
7 Easy Lessons
1-800-VICHY-44

White Flags
Be Seen and Live!
Latest Technologies
Store of Surrender
1914 Champs des Fromages

French Rifles!
- Mint Condition
- Never Fired
- Only Dropped Once

Jacques' Army-Navy Surplus
1940 Rue des Poulets

Seeking Married Men
Arranging the Finest Adulterous Affairs Since 1783
www.mistress-match.com

Seminar
Surrender or Run: Dichotomies in Modern Warfare
7 p.m. Derrida School of Certainty
Salle de Sartre

From Want Ads *Le Figaro* October 15, 2004

46

ALGÉRIE

> *Fight:* Algerian War of Independence
> *Date:* November 1954–July 1962
> *Opponents:* Fourth & Fifth Republic versus Front de Libération Nationale
> *Incompetent French Leader:* Ten different French Prime Ministers served during this period
> *Outcome:* French lose the war! French lose a colony! French lose a republic! French lose!

PATHETIC DETAILS:

France had been infesting Algeria for over one hundred years after subduing the local savages in a campaign that ran from 1830 to 1847. Of course, the problem with local savages, being savages, is that they generally refuse to recognize the superiority of their European colonial overlords and just never understand or accept where they belong in the pecking order, that being on the very bottom. Sheesh!

Being unusually dim savages, it took the Algerians about fifteen years after the Germans rolled through Paris to figure out that *les françaises*, revealed as physically weak by the Germans, Vietnamese, and Gaulladet School of the Deaf and morally bankrupt by the Vichy, were ripe for the picking. What they lacked in smarts, the savage Algerians more than compensated for with…. umm… savagery.

In November 1954, the Algerian *Front de Libération Nationale* (FLN) launched one of the most…savage wars since the previous savage war. French colonists, dismayed at the savage ingratitude of the oppressed indigenous population, found themselves under attack on all fronts. Men, women, children, house pets, nuns. Everyone was fair game. Nowhere was safe. These colonists, who often referred to themselves as *pieds noir* (so called because farm work left them with sunburnt, dirty "black feet"), resorted to their own savage counterterror tactics, which did not seem to differ too greatly from FLN's own savage terror tactics. Now, if you listen to the Frogs, they'll tell you that that the *colons* were called *pieds noir* because of their great love for the Algerian soil, which was won fair and square by butchering the local savages, who, since they did not call themselves *pieds noir*, clearly did not have the appropriate love for the Algerian soil. However, as we are all familiar with French standards of personal hygiene, well, we don't really need to say anymore, do we?

Unfortunately, for *les pieds noir*, their brethren across the Mediterranean in Frogistan had much less love for Algerian soil, though, they, too, showered once a month whether they needed it or not. Recognizing that the string of "not exactly victories" over the past fifteen years (Germany, Vietnam and Suez) constituted a clear trend and not just a momentary lapse, the tiff with the FLN quickly became unpopular (quickly meaning about two days into the fight). In their enthusiasm, some Frenchmen advocated surrendering the Alsace-Lorraine region to induce the Algerians to end the war. Calmer heads wisely advocated a delay in capitulating until the Algerians actually managed to land in France proper. Sadly, the Algerians never obliged.

However, the *pieds noirs*, especially the hardliners known as *ultras*, advocated a fight to the last conscript. Charles de Gaulle, who became president of the republic in 1958, had other ideas. Despite intense opposition to his plans for withdrawal (see below), negotiations with the FLN began in June 1960 that ultimately ended with the Evian Accords of 1962. Algeria was no longer a part of France.

NOTABLE EMBARRASSMENT:

With the war dragging on, the *pieds noirs* in Algeria grew impatient with the French government. Given the Gallic track record, they knew that the politicians would be looking for the back door before too long. Not surprisingly, the *pieds noirs* and certain army officers supportive of their cause began to think that, given the choice between tackling the FLN or the shaky-kneed politicos of the Fourth Republic, the latter would be, by far, the easier target.

However, all of this hushed conspiring and an active *coup d'etat* plot were put on hold when Charles de Gaulle ascended to the presidency of the brand spanking-new Fifth Republic, which replaced the snake-bitten Fourth Republic that had been built on the ruins of the ill-fated Third Republic that in turn scavenged the corpse of the Second Empire that… well, you get the idea. Surely, he was the sort of man who would take a firm stand in Algeria just as he had taken a firm stand against the ~~Germans~~ British and ~~Soviets~~ Americans. This line of optimism was bolstered when de Gaulle visited Algiers on June 4, 1958 and declared, *"Je vous ai compris."* ("I have understood you.") The gathered throng roared its approval, for meaningless declarations like this are powerful stuff with the French. Unfortunately, what de Gaulle really meant was "*Je vous ai compris, mais je n'aime pas vous.*" ("I have understood you, but I don't like you.")

Much to their credit, the *pieds noirs* quickly realized that they had been played for fools, and de Gaulle was bolting for the exit. By September 1959, de Gaulle publicly stated that it was time to offer the Algerians "self-determination." Time to dust off those *coup d'état* plans.

On January 24, 1960, a mob of colonists blocked the streets in the heart of Algiers. As two parachute regiments idly stood by, the *pieds noirs* defeated police sent to evict them from their barricades. It was a lot of fun (except for the policemen who were killed), but the paratroopers weren't ready to actually mutiny against de Gaulle and his government. The revolt of the colonists had expired stillborn.

However, that was hardly the end of the conspiring. When de Gaulle actually started talks with the FLN in June 1960, a number of generals hatched their own plot to ditch Charles de Gaulle. Their cause was bolstered when Air Force General Maurice Challe, formerly commander of all forces in Algeria and most recently commander of NATO Central Europe, resigned and threw in his lot with the conspirators.

Their hopes centered on the *1er Régiment étranger de parachutistes* (REP), the Foreign Legion paratroopers. The regiment would seize government facilities in Algiers, and this success would induce other Foreign Legion and regular army units to join the cause. On April 22, 1961, the plan was launched. The paras captured Algiers and the commanding general of French forces, Fernand Gambiez. Challe worked the phones, but the support never came. De Gaulle had the bigger megaphone, and his widely broadcast speech on April 23 probably convinced senior officers to avoid a lost cause because no one recognizes a lost cause like a French general.

By April 24, it was over. General Challe surrendered. The 1ᵉʳ REP retired from Algiers and destroyed their barracks. The mutiny, *c'est fini*. Yet another grand chapter in French military history had come to a close.

> "The Fourth Republic was arguably the most successful of all French republics except that it failed."
>
> —R.E.M. Irving, either being ironic, amusing, or clueless. You decide.

47

INDOCHINE

> *Fight:* French Indo-China War
> *Date:* 1946–1954
> *Opponents:* Fourth Republic versus Viet Minh
> *Incompetent French Leader:* General Henri Navarre
> *Outcome:* Mon Dieu! Quel désastre! (If that was in Vietnamese, that would have meant the Vietnamese had lost, but what were the odds that was going to happen?)

PATHETIC DETAILS:

With the end of World War II, the French and British both tried to get control of restive colonies that had either been under Japanese control (Hong Kong, Malaysia, French Indochina, etc.) or gotten uppity ideas about independence (Algeria, India, etc.). With all the recent lip-flapping about saving the world for democracy, defeating tyranny, blah, blah, blah, it made going back to the old colonial ways kind of tough. Chief among the wretched, unwashed, stinky natives all up in arms about this "Frenchie, go home and take me with you" agitating were the Vietnamese.

Vietnam had been thoughtfully swallowed up by France in 1887 as part of Indochine (comprised of Vietnam, Laos, and Cambodia), but the Vietnamese themselves had never been thrilled about it, the little, ungrateful, slant-eyed gooks. There had always been agitation against the French colonial administration, but it amounted to very little. However, the Japanese invasion in 1940 gave the Vietnamese the chance they were looking for. Leaders like Ho Chi Minh, a founding member of the French Communist Party, and his group Viet Nam Doc Lap Dong Minh Hoi (literally, "Me love you long time, Joe," but mercifully shortened to Viet Minh) resisted the Japanese, and, when World War II ended, they were in no mood to welcome the Frogs (defeated amphibians at that) back.

The Viet Minh had solid control of the northern part of Vietnam, while the Free French were able to grab the south. Fighting between the two sides broke out in early 1946. In one of the great ironies of world history, Ho Chi Minh sent President Truman a telegraph in February 1946 requesting aid against the French. Unfortunately for Ho (and for the United States), his Communist Party background was more than a minor impediment to garnering American support. While the United States would never commit troops (that mistake would come later on its own), some scholars believe that, by the end of the war, the United States bore 80 percent of French expenses in the campaign.

The war dragged on for eight years, growing in unpopularity the entire time. The French discovered that Vietnamese General Vo Nguyen Giap was a serious warrior and that, alas, they still weren't. Unlike the latter American involvement in Vietnam, the Viet Minh were often able to defeat

French forces in direct combat, most notably at Dien Bien Phu in 1954 (see below), which finally convinced the French to give up their erstwhile colony.

Notable Catastrophe: Dien Bien Phu
General Navarre inherited a real mess when he took the overall command of forces in French Indochina. He had only been on the job a short time when he pronounced the war unwinnable, but thought it desirable to get in one last victory. Perhaps, it was for leverage at the peace negotiations in Geneva. Perhaps, he was simply curious to know what it felt like to…you know…actually be victorious. It's sort of like living next door to swingers. It's not your cup of tea, obviously, but you're sort of curious what it's like to…umm, anyway, French Premier René Mayer (who may or may not have led a swinging lifestyle, but why do you have to drag the man's private habits into this?) had ordered Navarre to achieve a military result that would lead to an acceptable political solution to the conflict. On the other hand, maybe it was just typical Frog stupidity. (When in doubt, go with the obvious answer.)

Be it politics, polyamory, or pugnacity, Operation *Castor* was one of those plans that sounded like a good idea at the time. The French would parachute a battalion of paratroopers deep into Viet Minh territory, 175 miles west of Hanoi, ten miles from the Laotian border, and a million miles away from a happy outcome. The Viet Minh had been threatening Laos, and the garrison at Dien Bien Phu would cut the Vietnamese supply lines, making their position in Laos untenable. This remote outpost, also chosen because of the presence of an old airstrip, would be supplied by air (guess the French hadn't received the memo on Stalingrad from their German pals). On second thought, given that the Viet Minh had shown the ability and willingness to duke it out toe-to-toe with the French on the battlefield, it was a pretty idiotic idea. Navarre's subordinates were appalled by the plan.

The French paratroopers easily gained control of the valley at Dien Bien Phu as nine thousand troops dropped in on November 20, 1953. The French quickly fortified their positions and gave them hard-fighting names like "Claudine," "Beatrice," "Gabrielle," and "Isabelle." Allegedly, these were the names of commanding officer Colonel Christian de Castries's former mistresses. (Note: unlike most everything else in this book, we're not making this part up, and it sort of ties in with the wife-swapping gag.)

Unfortunately, it didn't occur to them that the heavily wooded high ground surrounding the valley might pose a problem (Sounds sort of like that "Tanks can't get through the Ardennes Forest" thing that undid the Maginot Line). Perhaps General Navarre should have informed General Giap that he wouldn't be able to get his heavy artillery onto the heights surrounding Dien Bien Phu. Without that helpful reminder of the impossible, the Viet Minh somehow dragged their cannons up the hills. The stage was set.

On the morning of March 13, 1954, much to their Gallic chagrin, the French awoke to the soothing sounds of an artillery barrage. Even worse, the paratroopers also realized that they were now surrounded, and their positions were being pounded with no chance for counter-battery fire to silence the Vietnamese guns. The French artillery commander killed himself in shame.

The siege took fifty-seven days, but there really wasn't much to the battle itself. The Viet Minh methodically tightened the noose around the French, who were outnumbered and outgunned. Air supply could only do so much, and the monsoon weather badly affected incoming flights.

On May 7, Colonel de Castries surrendered his force. Two thousand, three hundred men had died. Eleven thousand, eight hundred more were marched off into a brutal captivity that killed over half of the POWs. Nothing had been achieved by the sacrifice. The French Indochina War was over. The United States should have paid more attention. A lot more attention.

> *"I am amazed—yes, that is the word, amazed—that France's fine expeditionary corps in Indochina is commanded by officers who would rather negotiate than fight."*
>
> —Admiral Georges Thierry d'Argenlieu commenting on General Philippe Leclerc's actions in Indochina. Clearly, the good admiral wasn't paying much attention to his French history. Thankfully, you dear reader, can buy this book on Amazon for a very reasonable price and avoid the admiral's terrible mistake.

40

FRENCH FOREIGN LEGION

From Article 7, Legionnaire's Code of Honor
You never surrender either your dead, your wounded, or your weapons.

Lieutenant Maudet leads the final bayonet charge at the Hacienda Camerone
(*Battle of Camerone – April 30, 1863* by Jean-Adolphe Beaucé)

It's true. There is a French Foreign Legion (*Legion étrangère*), and if there was ever a French fighting unit you would feel comfortable about covering your back, it would be the Legion.

The Legion got its start back in 1831 under the Orleanist King Louis Philippe when he needed help conquering Algeria, knowing he couldn't count on his own worthless countrymen.

Since that time, the Legion has been involved in virtually every conflict that France has been in and deservedly earned a reputation as a tough bunch that won't run in a fight.

Their first famous battle occurred during the ill-fated Mexican Adventure (see Chapter 33). An infantry patrol of three officers and sixty-two men led by Captain Jean Danjou was waylaid and trapped in the Hacienda Camerone by two thousand Mexican soldiers on April 30, 1863. Down to a handful of effectives, the Legionnaires launched a bayonet attack that earned the respect of their opponents, who commented, "They're not men. They're devils." The survivors were allowed safe passage and carried out the unit flag and Captain Danjou's body. Danjou's wooden hand is now a holy relic for the Legion.

During the schizophrenia of Vichy France versus Free France in World War II, rival Legion forces actually battled each other in Syria. Their last great action was in the dramatic defeat by the Viet Minh at the siege of Dien Bien Phu (see Chapter 47) in May 1954.

JOINING THE LEGION

Honestly, why?

All right. Here are the requirements to be a Legionnaire (from the French Foreign Legion website (http://www.legion-recrute.com/en)):

- Be seventeen to forty years old

- Be a male (sorry, Mesdames)

- Hold an official identity card (if you're an ax murderer on the lam, be warned: the Legion conducts background checks these days)

- Be physically fit for whatever duty may be required (leave it to the French to state the obvious)

- Knowledge of the French language is not required

You must then present yourself to a recruiting office in France on your own dime. There, you will be sent to the Legion HQ at Aubagne (near the southern port city of Marseille) to undergo a battery of tests. If you pass, then you get to sign your life away for five years and join the 7,700 legionnaires from over 130 countries in one of ten regiments posted around the vast French empire. We understand that Abu Dhabi is nice this time of year and that the 13th Demi-Brigade is a popular assignment. *Bon chance.*

"Sometimes it is tougher to fight my superiors than the French."

—Heinz Guderian, German general, developer of the armored tactics known as *blitzkrieg*

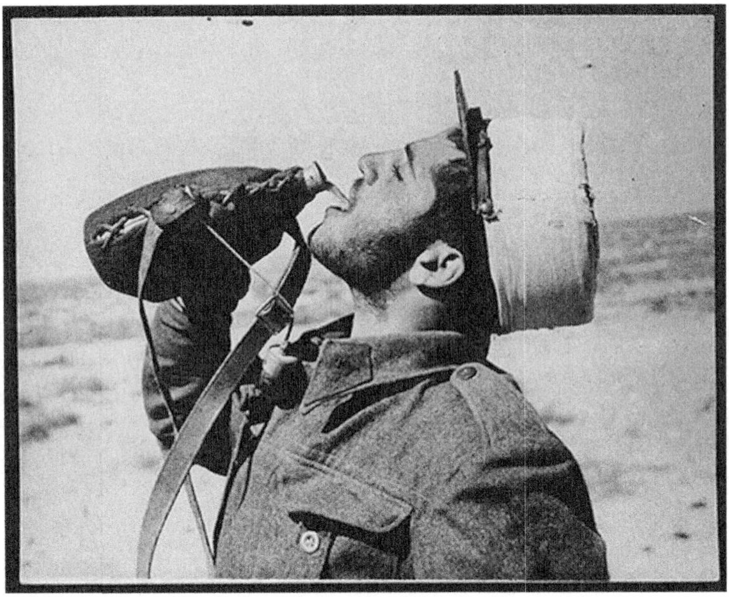

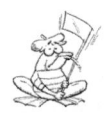

49

SUEZ

Fight:	Suez Crisis (Operation *Musketeer* or the 1956 Arab-Israeli War)
Date:	October 1956–March 1957
Opponents:	Fourth Republic Great Britain Israel versus Egypt
Incompetent French Leader:	Guy Mollet, Prime Minister
Outcome:	French slapped down hard.

PATHETIC DETAILS:

Now, don't misunderstand what we're about to tell you. We deplore peace just as much as the next fellow, preferring even the most squalid conflict over the dullness of tranquil calm. However, some wars are just so harebrained that it would be far better to just stay home and get fat watching hours and hours of bad French cinema.

One of those moronic squabbles was the Suez Crisis of 1956 that matched up the economic, intellectual, and military powerhouse that is Egypt against the trio of Great Britain, France, and Israel. Anytime you see countries that hate each other teaming up against a civilizational midget like Egypt, something's amiss. Anytime France is part of the mix, the chances of winning are about zip.

Obviously, the center of the big kerfuffle was the Suez Canal, which was then the primary route for oil shipments to Europe. (No blood for oil!) When the Egyptian Army overthrew King Farouk in 1952, Arab nationalists, led by Gamal Abdel Nasser, charted a new policy for the canal that quickly angered just about everyone in the region. Striving to achieve global annoyance, Nasser thumbed his nose at the United States by strengthening diplomatic ties with Communist China and purchasing Soviet weaponry. The Americans, in turn, cancelled financial support for the Aswan High Dam on the Nile River.

Perhaps Nasser was surprised by this, but, regardless, he needed another source of bucks to keep building that dam. In July 1956, he announced the nationalization of the Suez Canal (technically, the operating company of the canal), over 40 percent of which was still owned by British firms.

Now things started to get interesting. Obviously, the Brits were steamed. Not only did they lose money on the deal, but their economic lifeline now lay in the hands of a sleazeball that Prime Minister Anthony Eden enjoyed comparing to Mussolini and Hitler. They found an obvious, if unlikely, ally in the Israelis, also peeved by Egyptian meddling with their shipping at the port of Eilat. One can only assume that the French were included as a comedic foil just in case the operation was ever made into a movie.

During the double top secret meetings, the three parties developed Operation *Musketeer*. No word on which country got to be D'Artganan, but France no doubt filled the role of Shemp the Fourth and Forgotten Musketeer. The plan created was ingeniously simple:

Phase 1: Israel attacks Egypt

Phase 2: France and Great Britain intervene

Phase 3: Egyptian and Israeli armies cease hostilities and withdraw from either side of the canal

Phase 4: British and French forces deploy around canal, securing it for The Children™

Phase 5: Sharks with laser beams in their heads patrol the canal waters, ensuring safe passage of shipping

Phase 6: ~~While the foolish British are absorbed in Egypt, our armies will regain Canada and restore France to its rightful place as the greatest nation on Earth! Oui, oui, oui!~~

Except for Phase 6, it seemed like a great plan, and, for a few days after the Israelis launched *Musketeer* on October 29, 1956, everything progressed according to schedule (despite the presence of the French). The Israelis drove toward the canal, the Egyptians retreated like... well... Frenchmen, the Brits and Frogs offered their "services" and.... Nasser told them to pound sand, which in a place like Egypt might not actually be an insult.

Thwarted in their mission as honest, heart-felt peacekeeping intermediaries, who had absolutely no pecuniary interests in the canal (nope, none whatsoever), they settled for bombing the crap out of the Egyptians. And that's a good thing. Nasser responded by blocking the canal with sunken ships. What a jerk!

Even though the plan had gone awry, it was still a lot of fun. Good friends. Good times. Good target practice and no one was really getting hurt (except for the Egyptians, of course, but there's plenty more of that inbred Third World cannon fodder where they came from). Unfortunately, *Musketeer* did realize one significant accomplishment: the seemingly impossible feat of getting the Soviet Union and the United States on the same side.

The Russians rushed (man, that's poetic) to the diplomatic aid of its client state, undiplomatically threatening to blow everyone involved to kingdom-come. As for the Americans, world wars were now seen as bad for business. All of that Arsenal of Democracy blah-blah was pretty heady stuff until you realize that everyone else has skedaddled from the party and stuck you with the bill and a huge clean-up. Even worse, since the United States had just been criticizing the Soviet's crashing into Hungary, it would look really bad to not say something about what was happening in the Sinai.

President Eisenhower, being the sort of take-charge man accustomed to exterminating verminous world leaders (as opposed to certain unnamed affirmative action community organizers who think they can reserve a conference room and talk their opponents into submission), demanded the British and French call it quits. Knowing that he would get further with a kind word and a gun than merely with a kind word alone, he hinted that the U.S. Treasury might dump its pound sterling reserves, triggering a fire sale on the British currency. It was enough. The Europeans blinked. Eden was forced to resign.

Musketeer was effectively over with the last Israeli troops withdrawn in March 1957. The British Empire was kaput. France had just suffered its second colonial defeat and was well on the way to completing the trifecta in Algeria. If World War II had not spelled it out, this did: the power in the world now resided in Moscow and Washington, not in Paris (ha!) or London.

> "I have tried to lift France out of the mud. But she will return to her errors and vomitings. I cannot prevent the French from being French."

—Charles de Gaulle (no wonder they love him so)

50
GREATEST FRENCH WAR MOVIES OF ALL TIME

1. A Bistro Too Far

2. Apocalypse Tomorrow Or Perhaps the Next Day

3. Chicken Cordon Bleu Hill

4. We Were Never Soldiers, Not Even Once

5. Black Beret Down

6. Out of Harm's Way

7. Monsieur Roberts

8. The Bridge on the River Seine

9. Lawrence of the 13th Arrondisement

10. Red Badge of Ennui

11. Terms of Surrender

12. Saving Private François's Fromage

13. Retreat or Die

14. From Here to the Nearest POW Camp

15. The Wine Locker

> "The French want no one to be their superior. The English want inferiors. The Frenchman constantly raises his eyes above him with anxiety. The Englishman lowers his beneath him with satisfaction."
>
> —Alexis de Tocqueville

51

FROGS VERSUS ECO-FREAKS

Fight:	Sinking of *Rainbow Warrior* (Operation *Satanic*)
Date:	July 10, 1985
Opponents:	Direction Générale de la Sécurité Extérieure (DGSE, the French Secret Service)
	versus
	Greenpeace
Incompetent French Leader:	President François Mitterrand
Outcome:	Greatest French naval victory in two centuries!

PATHETIC DETAILS:

When the smelly, arrogant minions of La Belle France square off with the smelly, arrogant activists of Greenpeace, it's time to pass around the bowl of popcorn. For sheer entertainment, it can't be beat.

In the early 1980s, the French decided it was high time to do some nuclear testing in the South Pacific at their Moruroa test site. The yutzes at Greenpeace took a dim view of that and did their usual nonsense of sailing into restricted areas and making a general nuisance of themselves. One can't help but notice that the hippies at Greenpeace never try that crap with the North Koreans or Russians or Egyptians or anyone else who would just as soon gun them down as look at them.

Since deep down, the Frenchman hates freedom of expression and loves to slaughter the weak, it shouldn't be too surprising that higher-ups in the Frog government decided that Greenpeace needed to be sent a message.

That message came late on the night of July 10, 1985, in New Zealand. Two limpet mines ripped apart the hull of Greenpeace's yacht *Rainbow Warrior*. Sadly, only one enviro-nut was killed as the ship sank to the bottom of Auckland harbor. Somehow, two French DGSE agents were arrested almost immediately, and the entire plot soon came to light. Three other agents were seized aboard a yacht that probably transported the mines to New Zealand. However, the Kiwi Kops didn't have enough evidence and had to release the three miscreants, who allegedly sank their yacht and were spirited away by a French submarine. Okay, that's a pretty cool touch, even if it was the French doing it.

The aftermath was *très* embarrassing for the Frogs. Two agents in the hoosegow for manslaughter. Three others jugged for a spell. Forced to pay New Zealand NZ$13 million (about $43.27 American). Compelled to issue a public apology. *Quelle horreur*!

The two agents were soon transferred over to French custody and ended up serving less than three years of their ten year sentence. All agents involved in the plot remained in the service and received promotions. And why the heck not? Other than the small part about getting caught, that was some real nice work they did.

Once it became clear that approval of the plan came from President Mitterrand's office, Defense Minister Charles Hernu and DGSE Head Admiral Pierre Lacoste were shown the door. A small price to pay for France's greatest naval triumph in a long, long time.

> "France has no friends, only interests."
>
> —Charles de Gaulle

52

COMRADE, MY COMRADE

The bond between French fighting men is legendary. Consider the following true story from the Second World War:

Jacques and Maurice became separated from their platoon during the withdrawal from the Belgian border. This did not stop them from bravely retreating under their own initiative.

Suddenly, a German Mark II panzer broke through the woods and headed straight for them. Maurice immediately dashed away. Jacques, on the other hand, dropped his rifle, shed his pack, removed his boots and started to lace up a pair of tennis shoes.

"Jacques," cried Maurice, "there is no time for that. You'll never outrun that tank."

"*Mon ami*," replied Jacques, "I do not have to outrun the boche. I just have to outrun you."

> *"I eliminate from the list of promotions any officer whose name I have read on the cover of a book."*

—Marshal Patrice de MacMahon, loser at the Battle of Sedan, first president of the Third Republic, and deep, deep thinker, as quoted in *The French Army: A Military-Political History*

53

A LETTER FROM BOOT CAMP

13 Août

Cher Maman,

   I have been in boot camp pour 3 weeks now, and I have only now decided to write you. I know that my decision to join the army disappointed you greatly. "You are dead to me." Those were your last words to me.

   I feared that you had emotionally turned your back on me because I did not wish to work in the family's yogurt factory or become a clerk at the post office like Oncle Luc. However, one of my comrades tells me that peut-être you have been engaged in a bit of post-modern irony. As you know, I never did well with les grandes philosophes like Foucault or Derrida. It all seemed like nonsense to me at the time. If everything about us is a social construct, then it seems like I should be able to walk through a wall if the mood seized me. I know that my literalness always displeased you. As you used to tell me when I was 7 years old, "If you can't learn to deconstruct the patriarchal, capitalistic, oppressive social structures about you, then—" Actually, I can't remember what the rest of it was. Tant pis.

Allez. The Army has been nothing as I expected. I was given uniforms my very first day, but, when I asked about boots, the supply corporal tells me, "They will impede your progress." I do not complain, though, because the running shoes we wear are very comfortable. Later, when I inquired about a helmet, a sergeant tells me, "It will impede your progress." Most curious.

Life is very busy here at camp. We must be awake by dix heures. Ten o'clock! So early! Then, we only get an hour and a half to eat breakfast. The crêpes suzettes are nothing like yours, Mama, but, unlike home, they let us eat in bed. I know it sounds horrible, but one must adjust.

We are always exercising. Yesterday, we ran backwards for five miles with our hands in the air the entire time. That is when I get in trouble with the drill instructor. I asked when we were going to get rifles. It was terrible. All the other recruits laughed at me. The instructor yelled, "It will impede your progress!" Then, I made un autre mistake. I said, "But I thought—" I couldn't finish the sentence. Il a dit, "You're not paid to think, you little American Rambo! This training is designed so that you can survive on the battlefield!"

Now my squad calls me L'Américaine or Rambo or John Wayne or—quelle horreur—George Bush! You remember how I did not do so well on the bacc and complained how unfair it was to have your life decided by a single test taken when you were 15? Do you remember what you told me? You said that, once I left home, I could practice the Anglo-Saxon economic model to my heart's content, but not under your roof. Papa was so ashamed of me. He, too, said, I was comme américaine. Where do I get these silly notions that one can pursue one's own destiny? I know that Sartre is correct—I'm just an insignificant speck in the universe, and I should be grateful to have a Parisian bureaucrat making all the important decisions in my life. But, for some reason, I yearn for more. Undoubtedly, it is the pernicious influence of Hollywood movies. I still have that volume of Descartes that you gave me for my fourth birthday. I promise that I will eventually get around to reading it, but I am très occupé these days.

Eh bien. In addition to the horrible teasing of my comrades, I can hardly endure the work. Le déjeuner begins at 1:00 p.m. and we are only given two hours to eat our lunch. Unlike breakfast, lunch is horrible. The bread must be a day old, and the bouillabaisse? Pfui! No self-respecting poisson would be caught dead swimming in such swill. At least, the base has a decent selection of wine.

What I cannot understand is why we can't spend less time studying German and have a more civilized lunch. I can barely finish my fifth cigarette before the instructors storm into the dining hall screaming, "Allez-y! Be in the classroom in forty-five minutes, or we will cut your chocolate ration by a fifth!" Ah, the barbarism of the soldier! I've begun to realize that your comment was spiritual. It's a man's soul that dies when he wears a uniform.

So I must hastily go through two more cigarettes and tromp over to the lecture hall. Even there, I have no reprieve. I am routinely mocked as the others, while we are supposed to be singing the German national anthem, slip in words from the American "Star Spangled Banner." It is all directed at me. Of this, I am certain.

Right before dîner, one should have a moment of tranquillement, oui? Mais non! Today, we followed German with lessons about les américaines. I was very glad to learn the phone number of the American Embassy. They teach us to use this in case of...well, they did not exactly say, but it most certainly must be important. Our instructor said that all the top generals have the number memorized. We also learned phrases like, "Bonjour, stupid Yank! If you weren't so incompetent, you would have liberated my country by now." That did not seem juste à moi, and I said so. I should have known better. Now, they refer to me as Monsieur Disney. That reminded me of when I was younger and wished to see Mickey the Mouse, and you forbade it. Instead, you gave me The Stranger by Camus. I will read that after I finish Descartes.

We get only trois heures pour dîner, which normally would border on savagery. How is a man expected to properly digest his food, savor two bottles of wine, and chain smoke three packs of cigarettes in such a short amount of time? However, we are so fatigue by this point, we are almost grateful to be forced into keeping dinner so brief.

Not to be indelicate, Mama, but, by neuf heures, I am ready to sleep. Nine o'clock! Some of the men are so exhausted that they dismiss their prostitutes with barely a glance. Do not pity them, though. Cette femmes are experienced in the ways of the army and, thus, do not take the rejection personally. I am told that they are very well paid for their expertise.

Alors, I can no longer keep my eyes open.

Dit bonjours a tous!

Votre fils,

Jean-Claude

> "France has usually been governed by prostitutes."

—Mark Twain

54
SHIP OF FOOLS

It was meant to be the pride of the fleet, a demonstration of French naval prowess and technological know-how. Instead, it became a national embarrassment. A vessel that even the French defense minister Alain Richard admitted was an object of ridicule. The sailors onboard began to refer to *Charles de Gaulle* as "le bateau maudit" (the damned ship).

Let's have a look at this Gallic rustbucket with a handy comparison to an American *Nimitz*-class carrier alongside:

	FS *CHARLES DE GAULLE* (ORIGINALLY *RICHELIEU*) (R91)	USS *HARRY S. TRUMAN* (CVN-75)
Awarded:	1986	1988
Keel Laid:	April 1989	November 1993
Launched:	May 1994	September 1996
Commissioned:	May 2001	July 1998
Builder:	DCN (Direction des Constructions Navales), Brest	Newport News Shipbuilding

Propulsion:	Two K15 Pressurized Water Reactors, two shafts	Two A4W Pressurized Water Reactors, four shafts
Length:	858 feet	1,092 feet
Beam:	211 feet	252 feet
Displacement:	42,000 tons	104,000 tons
Speed:	27 knots	30+ knots
Crew:	Ship's Company: 1,150; Air Wing: 600	Ship's Company: 3,200; Air Wing: 2,480

The ship was cursed from the very get go. *Charles de Gaulle* was the pet project of President François Mitterand. The only problem was that Mitterand was not fond of Charles de Gaulle, the man, and the carrier was initially named *Richelieu* after the slippery cardinal who served Louis XIII as his indispensable chief minister. When Jacques Chirac, an ardent disciple of General de Gaulle, came into office as Prime Minister in 1989, he immediately fought to change the name of the vessel and prevailed.

During the 1990s, work on the ship was halted four times (1990, 1991, 1993 and 1995) because of budget shortfalls. Recognizing that the original goal of 1996 was as unrealistic as defeating the German Army, much less the German Boy Scouts, Jacques and the gang wisely chose to make *CDG* a millennium project. Unfortunately, they should have chosen the Year 3000 instead of 2000.

When this floating wreck started sea trials in 1999, it was quickly realized that the flight deck was too short to operate the American-made E-2C Hawkeye airborne early warning aircraft. Press reports are sketchy here, so it is difficult to tell what was more alarming to the French establishment: that their carrier was an expensive dud or that they were using American equipment. Nevertheless, an additional fifteen feet of flight deck was added (plywood is cheap), and *Charles de Gaulle* was free to proceed to her (his, its?) next calamity.

It didn't take long for disaster to raise its head. Further sea trials revealed that the reactor shielding allowed five times more radiation exposure to the crew than permissible (unfortunately plywood, while useful, has its limits). The reactors had been a source of difficulty from the beginning as French designers opted to use reactors meant for submarines instead of designing a power plant expressly meant for an aircraft carrier. In addition to the shielding problem, *Charles de Gaulle's* top speed of twenty-seven knots was five knots slower than the forty-year *Foch* that it was meant to replace. There is no word as to whether they ever considered adding sails or rowers to make up for this sluggishness.

As it would later turn out, sails or galley slaves would have been a grand idea. On November 10, 2000, as the ship was en route to Norfolk, Virginia, the port propeller broke and *CDG* had to beat a not-so-hasty retreat back to Toulon in Frogland. Investigations showed that the spare propellers were also faulty because of a manufacturing defect. Not surprisingly, the manufacturer had gone bankrupt in 1999. The mighty French Navy had to scavenge two propellers from the decommissioned carriers *Foch* and *Clemenceau*. This further restricted maximum speed to twenty-four knots. No word on whether they considered turning her into a paddle-wheeler at that point.

Other than all of this, *CDG* has been a huge success. So much so, that the French are talking about building a second nonnuclear carrier…with help from the British.

> "The best thing I know between France and England is the sea."
>
> —Douglas William Jerrold

The aircraft carrier Charles De Gaulle

55
IT AIN'T JUST US!

"Europe unites in hatred of French" by Henry Samuel in Paris (from *The Telegraph*, May 17, 2005):

Language, history, cooking and support for rival football teams still divide Europe. But when everything else fails, one glue binds the continent together: hatred of the French.

Typically, the French refuse to accept what arrogant, overbearing monsters they are. But now after the publication of a survey of their neighbours' opinions of them at least they no longer have any excuse for not knowing how unpopular they are.

Why the French are the worst company on the planet, a wry take on France by two of its citizens, dredges up all the usual evidence against them. They are crazy drivers, strangers to customer service, obsessed by sex and food, and devoid of a sense of humour.

The French
are revolting!

Si, like always.

> "Jet2.com condemns French strike action and calls for lazy frogs to get back to work!" and "It seems to me that either the air traffic controllers or the students run France at the moment."
>
> —Philip Meeson, Chairman and CEO of UK airline carrier Jet2.com with a memorable two-for-the-price-of-one takedown

56

BEST SELLING FRENCH VIDEO GAMES OF ALL TIMES

1. Duke Appease'em

2. (We're) Doomed III

3. Art of Collaboration: Vichy

4. Bass Fishing with Jerry Lewis

5. Fortress Maginot

6. Attack of the Mimes

7. Attack on the Mimes

8. Soldier of Surrender

9. Stratego: Commemorative White Flag Electronic Edition

10. D-Day: What Took You Stupid Americans So Long?

11. Grand Arson Auto: Disaffected North African Immigrant

12. Collaborator's Creed

13. World of Cheesecraft

14. Call of Shirking

15. Ultimate Panic

16. Mortal Kapitulation

> "Haven't the French done enough harm to the world by surrendering to the Germans so easily, without bothering us at such an ungodly hour?"
>
> —Ioannis Metaxas, Prime Minister of Greece, quoted in *Ten Days to Destiny: The Battle for Crete 1941*

Top-selling French Video Game

57

DO THE FROGS REALLY LOVE JERRY LEWIS?

In a word: *Oui*!

Hey, we're big believers of to each his own, and, if someone has to watch a Jerry Lewis movie, it might as well be them. However, given the general French snootiness toward American culture, many are quite suspicious that the Gallic preference for Jerry Lewis has to be some sort of myth—a fiendish American plot on the level of accusing Joan of Arc of being a drunk.

Consider the following, though. The prestigious French movie journal *Cahiers du Cinema* (okay, prestigious in France, maybe) dotes on Monsieur Lewis. For a magazine that normally only gives the time of day to directors with names like Fellini or Rossellini or Breeson, this says something. The following is how Lewis's movies fared in their rankings:

The Nutty Professor: #7 in 1963

The Family Jewels: #8 in 1965

The Big Mouth: #6 in 1967

Cracking Up: #10b in 1983 (10b? Really?)

And finally, Jerry Lewis received the Legion of Honor on his eightieth birthday on March 16, 2006. French Minister of Culture Renaud Donnedieu de Vabre referred to Lewis as "the French people's favorite clown."

Oh, brother!

> "Let us say all bad Americans go to Paris when they die."
>
> —Mark Twain

58
A FINAL TRUE STORY

Recently, a German tourist traveled to Paris, but, as he flew in from the United States, he had to go through customs. The *douanier* examined his passport and asked, "Occupation?"

The German replied, "*Nein, danke.* I'm only staying a few days. Maybe next time."

> "France has more need of me than I of France."
>
> —Napoléon Bonaparte, speaking for all of us really

Printed in Great Britain
by Amazon

14699592R00139